www.neilhallam.con

Rocking the Streets

2nd edition

Published by Lauman Media and Publishing

Other titles by Neil Hallam

The Nev Stone & the Watchers novels

Between stone and a Hard Place

Stone, Paper, Bomb

Breath becomes Stone

Loxley: modern day Robin Hood tales

Loxley: a dish served cold

A biographical novel about my father's career

The Tricycle Spy (coming soon)

Other non-fiction titles

Mofos: a history of British motorcycle culture

www.neilhallam.com

About the author

Neil Hallam is a freelance photojournalist based in Nottingham, England. A keen motorcyclist throughout his adult life, Neil contributes to motorcycle magazines in: Australia, USA and Great Britain.

Neil's love of adventure has taken him to many of the world's most interesting places, which find their way, via his imagination, to the pages of his books. Many of his adventures have been on expeditions to remote areas including the Himalayas and Mongolia.

For over twenty years, Neil has worked in a variety of roles across the Blue Light Services. He has an MSc in Disaster Management and is a full member of the Emergency Planning Society. The real life experience and advanced theoretical understanding add depth to Neil's plot lines and subject matter knowledge

Rocking the streets

How music accompanied Britain's youth and gang culture

Introduction

This book grew directly from my first non fiction project; Mofos; a history of English biker culture. Through researching the various two wheeled sub cultures, I saw that alongside most of them ran an accompaniment of contemporary music.

The Rockers first had Rock & Roll and Rockabilly, moving later towards Heavy Rock. The Mods began with Modern Jazz, moving through Ska to eventually become Skinheads. The 1980's saw some very weird and wonderful fashions in both dress and music. The Hillbilly looking Hipsters of the early 21st century are said to have drawn their inspiration from the early Beatnik culture, which in turn, was part of the American music scene.

The current street gang and drug dealing culture has its own accompaniment of Rap. This has changed greatly over the decades, from a peaceful, happy form of black music, to the violent, gangster focused Rap of today. The lyrics often glamorise guns, drugs and violence. They denigrate women to little more than "ho's" or whores and the rhythm itself appears to promote violence (but that is what parents said of 1950s Rock & Roll).

In this project I combine my research with first hand experience of many of the youth cultures, beginning with my own teenage years in the 1970s.

My first bit of teenage rebellion came as a Teddy Boy, moving through Rockabilly into my adult life as a Biker.

While earning my way through college as a nightclub bouncer, I experienced many more of the changing youth cultures in Mansfield, my East Midlands home town. Then, during close to 25 years of police service, I have seen another two and a half decades of tensions between groups of youngsters experiencing the agony of growing up.

Part 1 - the 1800s

Chapter 1.1
The Scuttlers

By starting this book with the Scuttlers, I am immediately contradicting my assertion that music provided an identity to the gang culture of our young. Their heyday of the 1870s was well before gramophone records or the radio. But the period was not without music and I have included it as an important building block of the gang cultures.

The 'Scuttler' street fighting gangs of Manchester date from the mid to late 19th century, born in the harsh city environment in which the young men lived and worked. Just like the gangs of later centuries, the Scuttlers struck fear in the adult Population of the day.

The Scuttlers were a product of Manchester's slums, which grew in the 19th century, as thousands came from around Britain to work in its booming factories. Despite the huge wealth generated by factory owners, the Manchester working classes suffered long hours for low wages, with poor housing and diets. Yet this did not discourage an excitement for life on the streets of Ancoats and the other slum districts. Music halls, pubs and gin shops did a roaring trade, which was complemented by a lively street culture of people congregating on the streets to talk, drink, gamble and fight.

At the time, a fair fight was a legitimate means of resolving a dispute and the police rarely investigated unless the fight went sour. To a point, Scuttling had its roots within this culture and its street life of fighting.

The youngsters of Manchester regularly saw their fathers fighting. But the trigger for the younger generation's Scuttling rose from interest in the Franco-Prussian War by the boys of Ancoats. Young boys re-created the battles on the streets, using the sides of Catholic French and Protestant Prussian to reflect their own differences of Irish Catholic and English Protestant. This game quickly grew into a widespread fashion for street battles, beginning with the Rochdale Road War of 1870. This first flurry of street fighting laid the ground for the more complex culture of Scuttling. The battle lines between Catholic and Protestant reflected the geographical boundaries of streets and canals, as well as the clustering of different ethnic and religious groups.

The gangs forged strong group identities and gained power through local allegiances and bonds of friendship, advertised through careful dress. The gangs developed a distinctive dress code of long 'donkey' fringes, neckerchiefs, clogs and caps tilted back on the head. The clothing and accessories immediately identified the Scuttler, but also had violent functions, like the Scuttlers' belts, with their large buckles, which doubled as weapons. While the fashions were common to all Scuttler gangs, geography was the biggest influence in shaping Scuttler identity and the relationships between gangs. Gangs associated with particular streets or districts and policed their own territory. Gang members kept an eye out for men straying into their area; just being in the wrong place at the wrong time could lead to violence. It was not just men that these rules applied to.

Gangs expected the women of their area to court young men from the same area; this was frequently a cause of violence between gangs from Ancoats and Angel Meadow in 1886.

The gangs were admired, feared and loathed by the surrounding communities. The gangs were both violent and volatile. Feet, fists, knives, buckles, stones and even paving slabs were used as weapons. Fights often caused serious injury or death. Violence between gangs and bystanders could erupt for the smallest reason. Passers by could find themselves on the receiving end of a beating for bumping into a Scuttler or for appearing affluent or vulnerable. Even intervening to break up a fight between Scuttlers was rewarded with violence. Others suffered damage to their property, or had to alter their daily lives to avoid the Scuttlers.

The presence of Scuttlers created fear amongst the adult population, who were well aware of how violence could erupt at any time. Young gang members applied a different purpose to the street, by using it as a place for fighting.

Scuttling was a temporary phase in the lives of the young men of the gangs. Although the young Scuttlers were wild and undisciplined, many grew up in strict homes and had to contribute towards the family income. Before marriage, the family home was a place of constraint. When Scuttlers went to court, mothers rather than fathers attended. Mothers went to plead for their sons' good character, partly as fathers were at work, but also to convince the judges that sending their sons to prison would reduce the family income.

The stakes rose for the young men when they married and found themselves running their own homes. A prison sentence could literally put their wife and children in the workhouse. The excitement of street fighting had to be balanced against the cost to their family.

One of the nails in the coffin of the Scuttler was the growth of the youth club movement. Whilst another, was the popularity of football in the 1880s and 1890s. This was accompanied by aggressive policing and tougher prison sentences. The police had found it difficult and dangerous to prevent and control outbreaks of Scuttler violence. So, they changed their tactics and methods of detection. The Magistracy also noted the popular distaste for Scuttling incidents and used punitive sentences as a means of taking gang members off the streets and sending a message that scuttling would not be tolerated by the community. Prison sentences had a disruptive influence on gang leadership, but were not always a deterrent to the Scuttlers.

In recent years we have seen intense media interest in 'gang violence on the streets of London and other major cities. There are parallels between the Scuttlers and these more modern street gangs.

The gangs of both eras were not participating in thefts or any form of organised crime, but rather the gang was a way of finding friendship and a group identity. Much of their violence was directed at other gangs straying into their territory, in a similar fashion to so-called postcode wars in the 21st century. The Scuttler violence was heavily physical, using fists and knives, with reputations won and lost in the fights. These aspects found their parallels in a number of subsequent youth cults; strongly suggesting that group violence has a particular role in the social development of young men,

While the Scuttlers were battling it out in Manchester, another similar phenomenon was happening in Birmingham. The Birmingham gang achieved recent fame through a BBC drama series. *The Peaky Blinders* were a criminal gang based in Birmingham during the late 19th and early 20th century. They were one of many urban youth gangs in the era.

The TV series uses an attribution for the name "*Peaky Blinders*" as coming from the practice of stitching razor blades into the peak of their flat caps, which were then used as weapons. While some undoubtedly did this, the real explanation is that "peakys" was a common nickname for the flat caps which were popular at the time. These caps had hard peaks, which when they hit someone or head butted someone on the nose while wearing one, caused their victim temporary blindness.

The BBC series, starring Cillian Murphy, premiered in October 2013. It followed a gang based in Birmingham's Small Heath area, shortly after the First World War. Many of the scenes for the show were shot at the Black Country Living Museum.

The gangs had a distinctive clothing style, wearing peaked caps, cravats and bell bottom trousers, in a very similar fashion to their northern counterparts. The Peakys added jackets with a line of brass buttons down the front, giving an added flair.

Girlfriends of gang members also had their own distinctive style: lavish displays of pearls, a well-developed fringe covering the whole of the forehead and a gaudy coloured silk handkerchief covering her throat.

The BBC portrayed the Peakys as a single gang, but it was actually a Birmingham term for a wider form of violent youth subculture. Manchester's Scuttlers were many individual gangs, described by the umbrella name Scuttler. In exactly the same way; Mods and Rockers described a phenomenon and not a particular gang.

The youth street gangs in Birmingham were known as "Peaky Blinders," but they were also called "Sloggers". The gangs attacked drunkards, often leaving them unconscious in the gutter. If they could not trip a man or knock him down, they kicked or used the buckles of belts, just like the Scuttlers of Manchester.

Philip Gooderson, author of *The Gangs of Birmingham*, said that the Peaky Blinders began as one gang but the term later became generic. An earlier gang known as the Cheapside Sloggers appeared in the 1870s, and the term "Sloggers" (or "fighters") was already being used for street gangs when the Peaky Blinders emerged at the end of the century in the Bordesley and Small Heath areas, both extremely poor slums of Birmingham.

Chapter 1.2
From Music Hall to Protest Song

The 1870s of the Scuttlers and Peaky Blinders was a decade where the only way to obtain music was as sheet music sold in stores, performed in Music Halls, or sung in homes. Many of the songs were cheerful ditties, intended to brighten the lives of their audience. Other songs were similar to the ballads of old, which told a story. But there was a genre of song which fits better with the street violence of Manchester and Birmingham. These are the Protest Songs

English folk songs from the medieval and early modern period reflect the social turmoil of their day. Ballads celebrating heroes like Robin Hood, from the 14th century onwards, are expressions of a desire for social justice. Although social criticism is implied in the songs, there was no overt condemnation of the status quo.

The civil and religious wars of 17th century Britain gave rise to the radical communist Diggers' movement and its own ballads. The most well known was the *Diggers' Song*, with its incendiary chorus: "But the Gentry must come down, and the poor shall wear the crown. Stand up now, Diggers all." The Digger movement was quite violently ended, so few of their overt protest songs have survived.

The industrialisation of the 18th and early 19th centuries was accompanied by several protest movements and an increase in topical social protest songs and ballads. An important example is

13

'*The Triumph of General Ludd*,' which built a fictional persona for the leader of the 19th century anti technology Luddite movement in the midlands cloth industry, which made explicit reference to Robin Hood.

A surprising folk hero immortalised in song is Napoleon Bonaparte. He was often the subject of popular ballads, many of them lauding him as the champion of the common man in songs such as the "*Bonny Bunch of Roses*" and "Napoleon's Dream." As labour became more organized, such songs were used as anthems and propaganda, for miners with songs such as "*The Black Leg Miner*", and for factory workers with "*The Factory Bell*".

As in later decades, the 1870s saw many songs which were intended to promote support for a political cause. This was the beginning of a musical genre which has continued influencing music into the modern world. Among the big things that inspired protests at this time was prohibition of alcohol in the USA. These included hits such as "*Sons of Temperance*" and "*Let Us Pass This Goodly Measure*". Some were militant and others sentimental, often singing from the perspective of the abused child of an alcoholic. On the other side of the argument were songs like *"Now Suppose You Pass This Measure*" and songs which showed children in Poverty while their parents attended temperance meetings. These were written to mock temperance. There were also songs which supported allowing women to vote, this became a theme in political songs such as "*Daughters of Freedom*! and *The Ballot be Yours*" These suffrage songs gained publicity in the United States. Political causes became a major theme in popular music for the first time in the 1870s, with the exception of campaign songs for candidates which were already a regular musical genre and remained so until the 1950s when they were replaced by television.

In Britain, the 1870s saw expansion of the Music Hall. Those who wrote music began more regularly for live performances. It was an era of light music. The popular composer G. H. MacDermott was known for his themes which were not considered appropriate at the time, which led many venues to ban his work. This was an important period of transition in English music as it moved from the focus on rotating pieces in performance to the era of the Gilbert and Sullivan operetta

Before Music Hall was given its name, similar types of entertainment had been happening for many centuries. Music Hall brought together a variety of acts which together created an evening of light hearted entertainment. The origins of Music Hall were in a number of institutions which provided entertainment in Britain during the 1830s. These were: The back room of pubs, where simple sing-songs gave way to the singing saloon concert; popular theatre, sometimes in pubs, but mainly at travelling fairs; Song & Supper Rooms, where affluent middle class men enjoyed a night on the town and Pleasure Gardens, where entertainment became increasingly low brow as the years passed.

By the 1850s, the entertainment function of pubs had moved into purpose built halls; these new premises retained the traditional ambience of the inn. The format of the show was unchanged: a chairman would introduce song and dance acts onto a simple stage, whilst trying to keep order with a gavel. In all cases, eating, drinking and smoking carried on throughout the performance. The audience, usually exuberant with alcohol, both heckled and joined in with their favourite songs and performers.

The growth of the Halls was quick and spread rapidly across Britain with the first great boom in the 1860s. By 1870, 31 halls were listed in London and 384 in the rest of Britain. The growth was not only in the number of halls, but also in their amenities and catering facilities.

The Victorian Music Halls played an essential role in influencing the interests of the public during the 19th century. During a time when there had been widespread social revolution in most of the Europe's lower classes, the new mass commercial culture of the Music Halls was used to control similar feelings of discontent and revolution in its working class audience. This role of promoting patriotism over radical politics and reform, did not draw attention to the difficulties facing the working classes but, instead, distorted the issues by reducing them to a humorous level.

From the 1870s onwards, as the Scuttlers and Peakys were fighting on the streets, the Music Halls were being manipulated by increasing levels of middle-class control, which sought to snuff out any form of working class political discontent. Instead of performing protest songs, they were used as a venue for propaganda, and instead of speaking for the people; the Halls influenced their political views through patriotic fervour and a focus on domestic life.

The unique relationship between the performers and their audiences gave the working classes a place that could unite them and form an identity. Instead of the revolutionary views feared by the middle classes, it was a heavily patriotic, conservative sense of self that was created. The focus of the working classes, which could have previously been directed to challenging their own circumstances, was re-channelled by the Halls middle-class managerial structure promotion of the Empire and the ideology of nationality.

By the 1880s, Music Hall song; which had previously been used to inform the masses of Britain's place in world affairs, now focused on the patriotic ideals of Country, Queen and Empire. For the masses, it was the music halls that sold them the ideology of the British Empire and the comic singers became the salesmen.

One of the most influential singers of the period was 'The Great Macdermott'. Well known through out his career, it was in 1877 that Macdermott achieved real notoriety with his pro-war song, *'We Don't Want to Fight,* 'which added the word 'jingo' to the English language.

'We don't want to fight but by jingo if we do,
We've got the ships, we've got the men, and got the money too!
We've fought the Bear before and while we're Britons true,
The Russians shall not have Constantinople.'

This song highlights the new patriotic class consciousness that was being promoted in the Music Hall, re-enforced through audio and visual methods. A popular device for rousing the combative tendencies of the audience was to use emblematic figures with flags of different countries. Those were hissed or cheered according to the audience's taste or prejudice.

The experiences of war made a lasting impression on the working classes, which was kept alive by its continual use in the Halls. By the turn of the century Music Halls were deliberately used as agents of propaganda to eradicate class antagonism at home and to promote a sense of nationalism. By the end of the Victorian era, the patriotic influence of the songs had become so great that all balance between cynicism and idealism had been lost. Through both visual depiction and the songs, the working classes were being moulded into a patriotic collective, to be called upon in times of war. Without the careful management they experienced, the Halls could have brought social revolution and a dynamic working class entertainment. Instead, entertainment was used to restrain and reduce any political unrest that existed.

A huge change in the influence of music on Britain's youth came with recorded music, which became more widely available. Records would fuel the growth of Rock n Roll as well as every music based fashion from the 1950s onwards. Recordings did not gain significant ground until 1925 when the electrical recording process was first commercially introduced.

Unfortunately, sound recording came too late for many first generation artists, like George Leybourne. However, at the turn of the 19th and 20th century some of the survivors such as Dan Leno, as well as younger artists, began to make recordings. Initially these were very expensive (you could buy 12 of the best seats in the house for the price of one record), but over time, prices fell and records became more affordable by the typical Music Hall clientele. Over the first 30 years of the 20th century many artists committed their songs and performance to record, which can still be heard and enjoyed today.

Attempts have been made at Music Hall revival in Britain, both in the 1930s and more recently with "*The Good Old Days*" which was something of a pastiche.

One thing that did change with the advent of recorded music was the balance between protest song and government, or middle class propaganda. We saw music turn from the simple story telling of the old ballads, to anti hero worship in the Robin Hood songs. Then the Music Halls grew out of working men's taverns, performing very working class music. Then with greater middle class ownership, the Music Halls became cheerleaders of British patriotism.

All of the above would have had some influence on the lives of the Scuttlers and Peakys, but it was never the bonding force that music gave to later generations. The 19th century gangs were bound by geographic location, while later cultures, like Mod or Punk, were based on a common taste in music and fashion.

Part 2 - The 1920s

Chapter 2.1
The Flappers

The 1920s were also known as the 'Roaring Twenties' and was a decade of contrasts. WWI had ended in victory; peace had returned and brought prosperity with it. American alcohol prohibition spawned the rise of organised criminals like Al Capone and the Mafia. The newly affluent middle classes on both sides of the Atlantic were pushing their society's pre war boundaries.

The mobsters influenced the fashion of the time and eventually influenced the street gangs of today, while the hedonistic female "Flappers" heralded the notion of "girl power."

Flappers were a generation of young women in the 1920s who wore short skirts, had bobbed hair, listened to Jazz, and showed disdain for what was then considered acceptable behaviour. Flappers were thought brash for wearing excessive makeup, drinking, engaging in casual sex, smoking, driving cars and otherwise flouting social and sexual norms

The 1920s were a strange time. Everyone was glad that the War to End All Wars was over, but many people still lived in poverty. Children's toys were still homemade. Whip & top and skipping were popular pastimes. Carrot tops, turnip tops and wooden tops were whipped up and down the streets as there was little traffic. Comics such as "Chicks Own", "Tiny Tots" and "School Friend" were on sale for children.

In 1921 the Education Act raised the school leaving age to 14. Primary education became free for all children and started at age 5; all children were expected to attend for the full day from 9am to 4.30pm. In the countryside, pupils at some schools still practiced their writing with a tray of sand and a stick, progressing to a slate and chalk as they became more competent. Classes were large, learning was by rote and books were shared, because books and paper were expensive.

However, for some the war had been a very profitable time. Manufacturers of goods needed for the war effort had prospered and their owners had become very rich. Their children, who were now reaching maturity, became known as the Bright Young Things. For these youngsters from the aristocracy and wealthier classes, life was good. Nightclubs, Jazz clubs and cocktail bars flourished in the cities.

They were attention seeking, flamboyant, decadent, rebellious, promiscuous, irresponsible, outrageous and glamorous. These terms could easily describe the reality TV stars of today, but at the time it applied equally well to the 'Bright Young Things'. You could say they started the modern cult of celebrity. Chased by the paparazzi who were fascinated by their outrageous behaviour, the 'Bright Young Things' were the younger offspring of the aristocracy and middle-class people seeking to advance their careers through association.

What was the reason for this shocking behaviour? Their generation was too young to fight in the Great War. Perhaps their wild behaviour was a direct consequence of the war; the slaughter of so many young men had taught them to seize every day. Perhaps it was a reaction against the values of their parents. Maybe for the girls, their shocking behaviour stemmed from their new-found independence and confidence. Or, maybe it was a mixture of all of these things.

It all started with well-bred young girls and their 'treasure hunts' around London using public transport; buses, trams and tubes. They raced around London, running, shouting and generally making a spectacle of themselves. This led to young men becoming involved and the Bright Young Things started treasure hunting in fast cars, roaring around the countryside. These treasure or scavenger hunts evolved further, into weekend house parties, stunt parties and fancy dress parties. 'Bring a Bottle' parties were invented by the Bright Young Things at university in Oxford and Cambridge, as money was often tight for the students whose aristocratic families had been hit by death duties.

The party set were obsessed with Jazz which they saw as modern, raw and anti-establishment. They drank excessively and took drugs such as hashish, cocaine and heroin. They frequented the cocktail bars, Jazz clubs and night clubs of London where they danced and drank till dawn.

Petting became more common than in the Victorian era. "Petting Parties", where "making out," or foreplay, was the main attraction, became very popular, especially on college campuses, where young people "spent a great deal of unsupervised time in mixed company".

Just as today's youth subcultures have their own slang, so did the Bright Young Things, using words such as 'darling', 'divine' and 'bogus'. Men often behaved in a camp or effeminate manner, wearing makeup and flamboyant clothes. Although homosexual relationships were against the law in Britain in the 1920s, they were readily accepted by the Bright Young Things.

Perhaps the best known 'celebrity' of the time was Stephen Tennant, the youngest son of the Earl of Glenconnor. Outrageous in his dress and behaviour, he was said to spent most of his life in bed. His style was androgynous, rather like that of Boy George or David Bowie. He was constantly chased by the paparazzi. Elizabeth Ponsonby was the original 1920s 'It' Girl who partied hard and drank herself to death before she reached 40 years of age. Brenda Dean Paul was an actress called the 'society drug addict' by the press. In and out of rehab and prison, she reportedly 'lived on brandy cocktails and salted nuts for years'. Other members of the party set included Evelyn Waugh, John Betjeman, Noel Coward and Seigfried Sassoon the war poet. The press were fascinated by the wild behaviour of these young people. Some of the Bright Young Things used the press to further their own fame and notoriety; with some of their friends working for the tabloid press as reporters.

Somewhere along the line, the Bright Young Things became known as Flappers. There is a lot of speculation about where the name

Flapper came from. Some say it compared the Bright Young Things with a young bird flapping its wings whilst learning to fly. However, it more likely derived from an earlier use in northern England to mean teenage girl, referring to a girl whose hair is not yet put up and whose plaited pigtail flapped on her back; or even, from an older word meaning prostitute. The slang word flap was used for a young prostitute as early as 1631. By the 1890s, the word "flapper" was emerging in England as popular slang both for a very young prostitute and in a more general and less derogatory sense, for any lively teenage girl.

The word appeared in print during 1903 in Britain and 1904 in America, when novelist Desmond Coke used it in his college story of Oxford life, *Sandford of Merton*: "There's a stunning flapper." In 1907 English actor George Graves explained it as theatrical slang for acrobatic young female performers. The name was also used for a dancer, who danced liked a bird-flapping her arms while doing the Charleston dance move.

Flapper dresses were straight and loose, leaving the arms bare (sometimes with no straps at all) and lowering the waistline to the hips. Silk stockings were held up by garters. Skirts rose to just below the knee by 1927, allowing flashes of leg to be seen when a girl danced or walked through a breeze, although their style of dancing made any loose skirt flap up to show their legs. To enhance the view, some flappers applied rouge to their knees. High heels also came into fashion at the time, reaching 2 to 3 inches high.

Then, the Bright Young Things faded as quickly as they had arrived. The late 1920s saw mass unemployment and economic decline in

Britain. The wild and decadent behaviour of the party set became
distasteful; people became irritated by the excesses of this group
and the press became disenchanted with them. The Red and White
Ball in November 1931 was perhaps the 'party too far'. The dress
code was 'Red and White'; even the food was red and white. This
whole show of excess was received with hostility by the media and
signalled the end for the 'Bright Young Things'.

By the mid 1920s the post-war period of prosperity was well and
truly over. The re-introduction of the Gold Standard (where Britain
could only print as much money as the value of gold the country
owned) by Winston Churchill in 1925 kept interest rates high and
made UK exports expensive. Coal reserves were depleted during
the War and Britain began to import more coal than it mined. All this,
together with a lack of investment in new mass-production
techniques, led to a period of depression and decline in the UK
economy. Poverty amongst the unemployed contrasted greatly with
the affluence of the middle and upper classes. By the mid 1920s
unemployment had risen to over 2 million. The north of England and
Wales were particularly affected, where unemployment reached
70% in places. This to the Great Strike of 1926 and, following the
US Wall Street crash of 1929, the beginning of the Great
Depression in the 1930s. From a decade that started with such a
'boom', the 1920s ended in an almighty bust.

In America, popular contempt for Prohibition was a factor in the rise
of the flapper. With legal bars and cabarets closed, back alley
speakeasies became prolific and popular. This discrepancy between

the law-abiding, religion-based temperance movement and the actual popular consumption of alcohol led to widespread disdain for authority. But prohibition also gave birth to a much more dangerous and long lasting subculture than the Flappers.

Chapter 2.2
The Mobsters

Although this is a book about British youth and gang culture, it would be wrong to ignore America's influence on this side of the Atlantic. Today we worry about gangs of armed young criminals taking control of our city streets to ply their drug trade. But this also happened in 1920s America, where the commodity of choice was the newly outlawed alcohol.

Just as today's gangsters become glamorised by popular culture, through music and film, the Chicago mobsters of the 1920s also became a sort of folk hero. In Chicago there are gangster tours, a Tommy Gun's diner, speakeasies and they once had a sports team named the Chicago Hitmen. So it's easy to forget that these murderous lawbreakers introduced the world to concepts like the drive-by shooting.

The 1920s gangsters also wore fashion bought with the proceeds of crime and murder. 1920s America was a decade of: silk suits, diamond rings, guns, booze and broads. It also began the modern conception that gangsters and the criminal lifestyle are cool.

In the public eye, the 1920s gangster and bootlegger "outside the law" lifestyle brought money, fame, good clothes, attractive women, cars, and homes.

Read a book or watch a movie and the author or director will sweep you away in the romance of the gangster lifestyle and the criminal's code of honour.

Good quality, high fashion suits and accessories were as much the calling cards of the mobster then, as they are today. Along with the flashy suit, the twenties also gave us the best dressed and most famous gangster of all time: Al Capone. He wore a blue suit, with a white silk handkerchief, pearl grey spats and a diamond studded platinum watch chain. The 1920s also saw many other criminals with expensive suits and flashy names. The 20's most famous gangsters were: "Scarface" Capone, "Dutch" Schultz, "Bugs" Moran and" Lucky" Luciano. Every gangster had a colourful name to go along with his fine clothes. It has also been said that the gangster, as the public sees him, was a creation of the media. The tailored suit the gangster's uniform. They were avid consumers who invested time and expense to stay at the leading edge of fashion; fancy cars, tastefully furnished apartments, diamond stickpin, diamond rings, belt buckles, 50 suits of clothes and 25 pairs of shoes.

With the coming of prohibition in 1919, the 20s marked a huge shift in the way gangsters went about their business. No longer was it good business to beat someone over the head with a pipe to rob them of their watch and cash. Instead, the mob organised and integrated itself throughout the Chicago, Detroit, and New York. Bootlegging became big business for the most successful gangsters of the era. Some of them made millions each year supplying beer and liquor to the speakeasies around the country.
By becoming feared within their neighbourhoods the 1920s

gangsters earned a good living from the public: strong-arming them for small but widespread price increases for groceries and services, then skimming their profits. This way the gangster solidified his presence in urban culture and the criminal businessman was born.

The *Godfather* trilogy is Hollywood's expression of the "American Dream" come true: Vito Corleone came to America with nothing. He struggled to make ends meet through legitimate employment, pulled himself up by his bootstraps, organised a criminal mob of loyal followers and became wealthy and powerful. The Corleone family are poster boys for success outside the box. The 1920s gangsters became American icons of self-made-men.

Expanding their tentacles into illegitimate markets, like racketeering, bootlegging and prostitution, these gangsters lived life by their own dodgy but strict code of ethics and remained outside of the grip of the law.

1920s gangsters fashion owes its rise in the public's consciousness to the prohibition and the newspaper's love affair with these criminal media darlings.

Although their style is much more casual, today's gangsters remain ultimate consumers of anything luxurious and expensive. For the criminal businessman: jewellery, clothes, cars, and houses are the spoils of their criminal lifestyle.

But if the media's portrayal of the 1920s Chicago Mobster was all glitz and glamour, the reality was not always so glamorous. Scar Face Al Capone was one of the flashiest of Mobsters, but his fall

from grace was just as fast as his rise to power. Alphonse Gabriel
Capone, known by his nickname Scarface, was an American
mobster, crime boss, and businessman famous during the
Prohibition era as the co-founder and boss of the Chicago Mob. His
seven-year reign as crime boss ended when he was just 33 years
old.

Born to an immigrant family in Brooklyn, New York during 1899, Al
Capone left school after the sixth grade and joined a notorious
street gang, becoming accepted as a member. Johnny Torrio was
the gang leader and another member was Lucky Luciano, who
would later attain his own notoriety. Capone first became involved
with small-time gangs including the Junior Forty Thieves and the
Bowery Boys. Then he joined the Brooklyn Rippers and the powerful
Five Points Gang based in Lower Manhattan. During this time, he
was mentored by fellow racketeer Frankie Yale, a bartender in a
Coney Island dance hall called the Harvard Inn. Capone insulted a
woman while working the door at a Brooklyn night club and was
slashed by her brother Frank Gallucio. The wounds led to the
nickname "Scarface" which Capone hated. He was called "Snorky"
by his close friends, a term for a sharp dresser.

Capone indulged in custom suits, cigars, gourmet food and drink
and female companionship, which would eventually lead to his
decline. He was particularly known for his flamboyant and expensive
jewellery.

In 1920 Capone joined Torrio in Chicago where he had become a
lieutenant in the Colosimo mob. The rackets spawned by

Prohibition; illegal brewing, distilling and distribution of beer and liquor, were viewed as "growth industries." Torrio, aided by Al Capone, took full advantage of these opportunities. The mob also developed interests in legitimate businesses and cultivated influence with public officials, labour unions, and employees' associations. Torrio soon gained full leadership of the gang with the violent death of Big Jim Colosimo, and Capone became his strong right arm.

In 1925, Capone became boss when Torrio, seriously wounded in an assassination attempt, retired to Brooklyn. Capone built a fearsome reputation in the ruthless rivalries of the time. That reputation grew as rival gangs were eliminated and the suburb of Cicero became, in effect, a fiefdom of the Capone mob. Capone expanded the bootlegging businesses through increasingly violent methods, but his mutually profitable relationships with mayor William Hale Thompson and the city's police meant that he remained safe from law enforcement.

Capone revelled in attention, like the cheers from spectators when he attended ball games. He made donations to charities and was viewed by many to be a "modern-day Robin Hood".

The St. Valentine's Day Massacre on February 14, 1929, might be regarded as the last violence of the Chicago gang era, when seven members of the "Bugs" Moran gang were machine-gunned against a wall by rivals posing as police. The massacre was credited to the Capone gang, although Al himself was in Florida at the time. The killing of seven men in broad daylight damaged Chicago's image, as well as Capone's, causing influential citizens to demand government action and newspapers began to call him "Public Enemy No. 1". The federal authorities became intent on jailing Capone, and eventually prosecuted him for tax evasion in 1931, a federal crime and a novel strategy at the time. He was convicted and sentenced to 11 years in prison.

The FBI investigation of Al Capone arose from his reluctance to appear before a federal grand jury in March 1929 in answer to a subpoena. On March 11, his lawyers filed for postponement, submitting a doctor's affidavit which attested that Capone had been suffering from bronchial pneumonia in Miami, was confined to bed and that it would be dangerous to his health to travel to Chicago. His appearance date before the grand jury was re-set for March 20. FBI agents obtained statements saying that Capone had attended race tracks in Miami and that he had taken a plane trip to Bimini and a cruise to Nassau, that he had been interviewed at the office of his Solicitor in Dade County and that he had appeared in good health on each occasion.

Capone appeared before the federal grand jury in Chicago on March 20th 1929.

On May 17th 1929, Capone and his bodyguard were arrested in Philadelphia for carrying concealed weapons. Within 16 hours they had been sentenced to terms of one year each. Capone served his time and was released in nine months for good behaviour on March 17th 1930.

Meanwhile, the U.S. Treasury Department had been building evidence on tax evasion charges; in addition to Al Capone, his brother Ralph "Bottles" Capone, Jake "Greasy Thumb" Guzik, Frank Nitti, and other gang members were subject to tax evasion charges. On October 18th 1931, Capone was convicted and sentenced to 11 years in prison, fined $50,000 and charged $7,692 for court costs, in addition to $215,000 plus interest due on back taxes. After denial of his appeals, he entered the prison in Atlanta, serving his sentence there and at Alcatraz. On November 16th 1939, Al Capone was released, having served seven years, six months and fifteen days and having paid all his fines and back taxes.

It was while in prison that his life of excess and womanising came back to haunt him. Suffering from paresis caused by syphilis, he deteriorated badly during his imprisonment. Immediately after release he was admitted to a Baltimore hospital for brain treatment and then went on to his Florida home, an estate on Palm Island in Biscayne Bay near Miami, which he had bought in 1928. Following his release, he never returned to Chicago. He had become mentally incapable of returning to gang-land politics. In 1946, his doctor and a Baltimore psychiatrist both decided Capone had the mentality of a 12-year-old child. Capone remained on Palm Island with his wife and immediate family, in seclusion, until his death from a stroke and pneumonia on January 25th 1947.

Despite Capone's rather sorry end, his legacy has continued to the present day. The desire for glamour and to stand out from the crowd is nothing new; we get that from the animal kingdom, especially the birds. But the idea that being a "bad boy" is something glamorous is a very human trait. We will see that across many decades of youth culture, that violence often plays a part and particularly in modern gangs, criminality also goes hand in hand with membership.

Chapter 2.3

Swing, Dance Bands and the Charleston.

Throughout the 20s the two dominant musical genres were Jazz and the Big Bands. By the 1970s both had begun to lose their appeal with the young, in favour of what we now know of as Pop Music. But they both live on in small subcultures and both genres had a big influence on the music that was to follow them.

The Big Band sound was popular across both the 20s and 30s, even edging into the 1940s with American band leader Glen Miller entertaining the troops during WWII. But by the end of the war, the big band era was on the wane.

When Bandsman Bert Ambrose died in 1971, he was down on his luck. He was the manager of singer, Kathy Kirby, whose career was also in decline. He had once been one of the highest paid musicians in Britain, a Pop star before the term was coined. He performed every Saturday night on BBC radio and released countless records. But by 1971, popular culture had forgotten him.

Ambrose and his contemporaries in the 20s and 30s, such as Lew Stone, Jack Hylton and Ray Noble, were at the beginning of the 70s revered only by the nostalgic, and those for whom Rock & Roll and everything afterwards was an unlistenable racket.

These refined music makers from a bygone age had nothing to offer kids raised with electric guitars.

It's true that the British dance bands of the 1920s and 30s don't conform much to modern notions of what constitutes a Pop act.

They appeared more like orchestras: with a bandleader up front, often using a conductor's baton; musicians were divided into sections of rhythm, brass, wind and sometimes strings. Singers were essentially anonymous, their names rarely credited on the recordings. Yet they formed a soundtrack to British life and helped shape the Pop industry of today. Their existence coincided with the birth of radio and record companies, which freed musicians from their confinement to theatres and music halls, allowing Pop fans to experience their favourite songs at home without having to play them on a piano in their front room. The dance bands quickly realised the commercial potential of these new outlets, and exploited them fully. One of the more lamentable outcomes of this - savviness was a rush of novelty songs like *The Teddy Bears' Picnic* and *Makin' Wickey Wackey Down in Waikiki*. Equally prevalent were records of sentimental ballads like *Goodnight Sweetheart* and *Love Is the Sweetest Thing*, both written by Ray Noble. It is remarkable how little the ballad has changed in several decades since crooners like Bing Crosby.

In between these two extremes, the dance bands adopted many differing styles and a plethora of new songs. They worked ceaselessly: the top bands performed once a week on radio, but also each night in a West End hotel or nightclub, plus afternoons in the recording studio, recording up to 12 songs at a time.

If more American songs are remembered than British ones, it is partly because much of the dance bands' material was sourced from across the Atlantic. It is in their attempts to copy American music and particularly African-American music, that the dance bands most set a precedent for the future of British music. That started to become a problem when American musicians began to rethink their relationship with Jazz. Benny Goodman started the trend in 1935, when his band performed some 1920s arrangements by black musician Fletcher Henderson and so invented swing. This was the same process in which white singers in 1950s adapted black rhythm & blues songs and created Rock & Roll.

Swing heralded other developments. Young black musicians, exasperated by the colonisation of Jazz, evolved a more abstract music dubbed bebop; while on the other hand, singers who appeared with dance bands rebelled against their accessory status and started solo careers. This began the modern trend where the singer, not the band leader, is at the front.

British musicians wanted to respond to these changes, but as the 1930s rolled on, the growth of Nazism became a more urgent concern. The outbreak of war in 1939 did not stop to the dance band scene; as people still needed entertaining to keep their morale up. But it did put a pause on musical innovation. Even after the war ended, British Pop remained in limbo. New bands were formed, notably one led by Ted Heath, who had previously been a trombonist with Ambrose and Geraldo and many musicians clung to this existence for several decades. As the 1940s became the 50s, the only thing that changed in the Pop scene was the unstoppable rise of the singer. Sadly British audiences were not particularly enamoured with British singers, allowing yet more American influence into British music.

Week after week after its launch in 1952, the *NME* singles chart was packed with American acts. The exceptions: Vera Lynn, Dickie Valentine and Lita Roza had, just like their American counterparts, begun their careers with a dance band. No wonder Bill Haley and the Comets' *Rock Around the Clock* had such a massive impact on British teenagers when it arrived here in 1954: it was the first new sound they had ever heard.

There are still some big bands who tour the country, plus several independent labels specialising in reissuing dance-band material and web based radio stations that play nothing recorded after 1960. But some of the band music has had a striking effect on the mainstream. During the 1970s and 80s, film-maker Dennis Potter did much to revive interest in dance bands, with his 1978 TV drama *Pennies from Heaven*, where the nostalgic soundtrack of 1930s songs contrasted sharply with the show's dark storyline of adultery and murder.

Big Bands were by far the biggest musical phenomenon of the 1920s and they went onto have a huge impact on both music and culture for decades after, but there was a dance craze that suggests the Roaring Twenties more than any other dance. The Charleston was the signature dance of the Bright Young Things and the Flappers. It was named after the harbour city of Charleston in South Carolina. The rhythm was popularised in mainstream dance music by a 1923 tune called The Charleston which featured in the Broadway show *Runnin' Wild.* It became one of the biggest hits of the decade. *Runnin' Wild* ran from October 29, 1923, through to June 28, 1924. The peak time for the Charleston as a dance was between 1926 and 1927.

The basis of the dance probably came from the star, or challenge dances that in turn, were part of an African-American dance called Juba. The sequence of steps which appeared in *Runnin' Wild* was newly choreographed for popular appeal. At first, the step started off with a simple twisting of the feet to rhythm, in a lazy kind of way, similar to the Jay Bird step in Juba. But, when the dance arrived in Harlem, a new version was added. It became a fast kicking step, kicking the feet, both forward and backward.

Although it achieved its biggest popularity when the song *Charleston*, sung by Elisabeth Welch, was included in *Runnin' Wild*, the dance itself was first introduced in Irving C. Miller's Liza in 1923. Some writers claim that the dance was known well before that; in particular, a version was performed by Russell Brown under the name of the *Geechie Dance*.

The characteristic Charleston beat, which composer James P. Johnson said he first learned from Charleston dockworkers, incorporated the clave rhythm. Johnson actually recorded several versions of the Charleston, which in later years he derided as being of "that same damn beat." Many of these were recorded on player piano rolls, which have survived to this day.

The Charleston and similar dances such as the Black Bottom which involved kicking up your heels were popular towards the end of the

1920s. They became less popular after 1930, possibly because after seven years of being fashionable people simply became bored. The new fashion for floor length sheath evening dresses was also a factor. The new dresses constricted the leg movements needed for the Charleston. There is a British Pathé Instructional film from 1933 in which a new version called the Crawl Charleston, is demonstrated by Santos Casini and Jean Mence. This shows a very sedate version, similar to a Tango or Waltz. It wasn't until hem lines rose again at the end of the 30s that the Charleston was again seen in film.

A slightly different form of Charleston became popular in the 1930s and 1940s and is associated with Lindy Hop. In this later form, the hot Jazz timing of 20s Charleston was adapted to suit the swing Jazz music of the 30s and 40s. This style of Charleston had many common names, though the most used are Lindy Charleston, Savoy Charleston, 20s Charleston and Swinging Charleston. In all of these versions, the basic step takes eight counts and is danced either alone or with a partner. Today Charleston is an important part of the Lindy Hop dance culture, danced in many permutations: alone (solo), with a partner, or in groups of couples or solo dancers. The basic step allows for a huge range of variations and improvisation. Both the 20s and Swinging Charleston styles remain popular today, though swinging Charleston is more often integrated into Lindy Hop dancing.

Although parts of America were becoming very violent through the rise of the Mob, Britain in the 20s was a more peaceful place. Inhibitions were fading, probably due to the feel good factor of surviving the Great War. Particularly for the well off, life was more decadent. There were regular dances, held in purpose built dance halls, or small village halls. But there was no widespread Teen Culture, in fact the idea and the term Teenager, had yet to be invented. Scuttling had all but died out; it's origins in re-enactment of the Franco - Prussian Wars having been eclipsed by WWI. But worse was yet to come.

Part 3 - The 1940s

Chapter 3.1
The Zoot Suits

The 1940s produced the first cultural group to be immediately identifiable by its distinctive dress. The Scuttlers and the Peakys had their caps and the Flappers their short dresses, but these were really just the fashions of their day. The Zoot Suits, however, were a much more distinct group. They were predominantly an American phenomenon, but I have included them, due to the massive influence that American culture has had in our own country.

During the 1930s, Dance Halls were popular venues for socialising, dancing and forgetting the economic stresses of the Great Depression. Nowhere was this more noticeable than in the Manhattan district of Harlem.

Style conscious Harlem youngsters began wearing loose fitting clothes that accentuated their dance movements. Men wore baggy trousers, long jackets and hats ranging from porkpies and fedoras to wide-brimmed sombreros.

The image of these so-called Zoot Suits spread quickly and became popularised by performers such as Cab Calloway, who, in his *Hepster's Dictionary*, called the Zoot Suit "the ultimate in clothes. The only truly American civilian suit."

As the Zoot Suit became more popular among young men in

American minority communities, the clothes developed a somewhat racist reputation. Latino youths in California were known as "pachucos," who wore flashy Zoot Suits, porkpie hats and long watch chains, were increasingly seen by affluent whites as street thugs, gang members and juvenile delinquents.

Wartime patriotism didn't help matters either: After the bombing of Pearl Harbour and the American entry into World War II, wool and other textiles became subject to strict rationing. The U.S. War Production Board regulated production of civilian clothing containing; silk, wool and other essential fabrics. Despite these wartime restrictions, many bootleg tailors in Los Angeles, New York and other American cities, continued to make Zoot Suits, which used huge amounts of fabric. Servicemen and many other people viewed the oversized suits as an unpatriotic waste of resources. The local media was also happy to fan the flames of moral outrage: On 2nd June 1943, the *Los Angeles Times* reported: "Fresh in the memory of Los Angeles is last year's surge of gang violence that made the Zoot Suit a badge of delinquency. Public indignation seethed as warfare among organised gangs of marauders, prowling the streets, brought a wave of assaults and murder."

With its super-sized shoulder pads, sprawling lapels and peg leg trousers, the Zoot Suit grew out of the Drape suits popular in Harlem dance halls of the mid-1930s. The flowing trousers were tapered at the ankles to prevent jitterbugging couples from being tripped up while they twirled. By the 40s, Zoot Suits were being worn by men in working-class minority neighbourhoods across America. Though the

Zoot Suit was worn by the likes of Dizzy Gillespie and Louis Armstrong, it was not a just costume from the entertainment world, the Chicago trumpeter and clothier Harold Fox once said. "It came right off the street and out of the ghetto." Fox was one among many, from Chicago to Harlem to Memphis, who tried to take credit for inventing the Zoot Suit. The term came out of African American slang, but it was actually unbranded and illicit: There was no single designer linked with the look, no department store where you could buy one. These were ad hoc outfits, they were regular suits bought two sizes too large and then creatively tailored to a dandyish effect. Zoot Suits usually featured a watch chain dangling from the belt to the knee or below, then back up to a side pocket.

The trousers were known as pegged pants; trousers cut full in the waist and thigh area and tapering down to a cuff, or gather at the ankle. Some pegged pants included a full cuff with buttons; others were simply gathered around an elastic band. This style again became popular in the 1950s and 1980s.

It was common for a woman accompanying a man wearing a Zoot Suit to wear a flared skirt and a long coat.

To some men, the suit's ostentatiousness was a way of refusing to be ignored. The outfit had "profound political meaning," wrote Ralph Ellison, author of Invisible Man. "For those without other forms of cultural capital, fashion can be a way of claiming space for yourself." A young Malcolm X described the Zoot Suit as: "a killer-diller coat with a drape shape, reet pleats and shoulders padded like a lunatic's cell."

There were already tensions about the wearing of a Zoot Suit, as their mostly minority wearers were viewed as thugs and delinquents. With the additional problem of cloth rationing, they became a target waiting to be hit.

It was June 1943 when the Zoot Suit Riots broke out. For over a week, U.S. soldiers and sailors roamed Los Angeles beating up allegedly "unpatriotic" Mexican-American men, identifiable by their Zoot Suits. It was, as historian Kathy Peiss wrote in *Zoot Suit: The Enigmatic Career of an Extreme Style*, "perhaps the first time in American history that fashion was believed to be the cause of widespread civil unrest."

Tensions ran high between the Zoot Suiters and the big contingent of sailors, soldiers and Marines stationed in and around Los Angeles. Although Mexican Americans were serving in the military in high numbers, many servicemen viewed Zoot Suit wearers as draft dodgers; though many were actually too young to serve in the military.

On 31st May a clash between uniformed servicemen and Mexican American youths resulted in the beating of an American sailor. Partly in retaliation, on the evening of 3rd June 50 sailors from the local Naval Reserve Armoury marched through downtown Los Angeles carrying clubs and other weapons, attacking anyone wearing a Zoot Suit.

In the days that followed, the atmosphere in Los Angeles exploded in a number of full-scale riots. Mobs of servicemen took to the streets and attacked Latinos, stripping them of their suits, leaving them bloodied and half-naked on the street. Local police officers often watched from the sidelines, then arrested the victims of the beatings.

Thousands more servicemen, off-duty police officers and civilians joined the disorder over the next few days, marching into cafes and movie theatres, beating anyone wearing Zoot Suits or their favoured hairstyle, the duck-tail, which they often cut off.

By 7th June the rioting had spread from downtown Los Angeles into Watts, East Los Angeles and other neighbourhoods. Taxi drivers offered free rides to servicemen into rioting areas and thousands of servicemen and civilians from San Diego and other parts of Southern California converged on Los Angeles to join in with the beatings.

Leaders of the Mexican American community asked State and local officials to intervene, but their pleas met with very little action. One eyewitness, the writer Carey McWilliams, painted a terrifying picture: "On Monday evening thousands of Angelenos turned out for a mass lynching. Marching through the streets of downtown Los Angeles, a mob of several thousand soldiers, sailors and civilians, beat up every Zoot Suiter they could find. Street cars were stopped while Mexicans, Filipinos and Negroes, were yanked out of their seats, pushed into the streets, and beaten with a sadistic frenzy."

Local papers described the attacks as a vigilante response to an immigrant crime wave and police mainly restricted their arrests to any Latinos who fought back. The riots didn't die down until 8th June, when military personnel were finally barred from leaving their barracks.

The Los Angeles City Council issued a ban on Zoot Suits the next day. Amazingly, no one was killed during the week long riot, but it wasn't to be the last outburst of Zoot Suit related violence. Similar incidents occurred the same year in cities such as Philadelphia, Chicago and Detroit.

A Citizens' Committee was appointed by Governor Earl Warren, of California to investigate the Zoot Suit Riots in the weeks after the trouble. The committee's report found that, "In undertaking to deal with the cause of these outbreaks, the existence of racial prejudice can not be ignored." Also, the committee described the problem of juvenile delinquency as "one of American youth, not confined to any racial group. The wearers of Zoot Suits are not all persons of Mexican descent or criminals. Many young people of today wear Zoot Suits."

The Zoot Suit lives on in film and stage. *Zoot Suit* is a 1981 film adaptation of the Broadway play with the same name. Both the play and film were written and directed by Luis Valdez. The film stars Daniel Valdez and Edward James Olmos (later to star in *Miami Vice*) both reprising their roles from the stage production, along with Tyne Daly (from *Cagney & Lacey*). Many other cast members from the Broadway show also appeared in the film. Like the play, the film also features music from Daniel Valdez and Lalo Guerrero, the "father of Chicano music."

In *Zoot Suit*, Luis Valdez tells a story involving the real-life events of the Sleepy Lagoon murder trial; where a group of young Mexican-Americans were charged with murder, which resulted in the racially fuelled Zoot Suit Riots in Los Angeles. In the play, Henry Reyna (inspired by the real-life defendant Hank Leyvas) is a pachuco gangster. He and his gang, were allegedly unfairly prosecuted and were thrown in jail for a murder they did not commit. The play is set in the barrios of Los Angeles during the early 1940s against the backdrop of the Zoot Suit Riots and WW II. Just as he did in the play, Edward James Olmos played El Pachuco, an idealized Zoot Suiter, who functioned as the narrator throughout the story and serves as Henry's conscience.

A Zoot Suit also played a staring role in the 1994 film, *The Mask*, an American fantasy comedy based on the comic series of the same name in Dark Horse Comics. The film stars Jim Carrey and Cameron Diaz in her film debut. It tells the story of an unlucky bank clerk, who finds a mask that grants the wearer cartoon-like superpowers. Carrey's character, Stanley Ipkiss was a shy bank clerk working at the Edge City bank. He was frequently ridiculed by everyone around him, except for his best friend Charlie Schumaker and his Jack Russell Terrier Milo. Meanwhile, Dorian Tyrell, the gangster owner of the Coco Bongo nightclub, plots to overthrow his boss Niko. One day, Tyrell sends his singer girlfriend Tina Carlyle into Stanley's bank to scope its layout, in preparation to rob the bank. Stanley is attracted to Tina, and she appears to reciprocate. Unable to enter the Coco Bongo to watch Tina perform, Stanley wanders towards the city's harbour, where he finds a wooden mask. Putting it on his face, the mask transforms him into a green-faced, Zoot Suited, wisecracking trickster called the Mask, who is able to cartoonishly alter himself and his surroundings at will. Stanley exacts revenge on his tormentors and scares off a street gang that attempts to rob him, by creating a Tommy gun from a balloon.

Today, genuine 1940s Zoot Suits have become almost mythically difficult to obtain. Many were lost through rioters slashing them to ruins, but the more likely reason for their disappearance after the craze faded in the 50s was less dramatic; most were simply remade into other garments. Original specimens are very hard to come by: It took curators from LACMA more than a decade to find one, and when they did, in 2011, it cost them just under $80,000, an auction record for an item of 20th century menswear.

But the suit had a successful afterlife, influencing styles from Canada and France to South Africa and the Soviet Union.
The Zoot Suit was the subject of the Who's first single. Although the group used the name The High Numbers, to release their single; *Zoot Suit / I'm the Face*. Their first single under the Who moniker was *I can't Explain*.
The outfit's iconic shape was also taken up in the '80s by Japanese avant-garde designers, who sent models down the cat walk in them, around the same time that MC Hammer began wearing his drop-crotch trousers; causing outrage over the supposed immorality of sagging pants.
During the late 90s a record called "Zoot Suit Riot," by the swing-revival band the Cherry Poppin' Daddies, became a hit. But by then the suit's origins had largely been forgotten. No longer was the Zoot

Suit evocative of the power of fashion for the disenfranchised, it had become a historical oddity known by a charming name.

Chapter 3.2
Bebop

Throughout the 40s, music remained what it had been for several decades, something to dance to. Dance Halls were still one of the only available entertainment venues. The Big Band had survived several offshoots, mostly Jazz based. But the groups who expressed themselves by wearing Zoot Suits, also wanted to stamp their own identity onto their music. This is where Bebop began to develop.

Bebop or Bop is a style of Jazz developed in the 1940s in America. It features songs characterised by a fast tempo, complex chord progressions with rapid chord changes and numerous changes of key, along with the all important improvisation.

Bebop developed as the younger generation of Jazz musicians expanded the creative possibilities of Jazz. They moved beyond the popular, dance-oriented swing style to a new "musician's music" that was not as easy to dance to and demanded close listening. Because Bebop was not intended for dancing, it allowed the musicians to play at faster tempos.

Bebop groups rhythm sections benefited, as the new groups greatly expanded their role. Where the main ensemble of the swing era was the Big Band, with up to fourteen players, the classic Bebop group was a small combo that consisting only of saxophone, trumpet, piano, double bass, and drums playing music in a supportive role for soloists. Rather than play heavily arranged music, bebop musicians typically played the melody of a song, called the "head," with accompaniment from the rhythm section, followed by a section in which each of the performers improvised a solo and then returned to the melody at the end of the song.

Some of the most influential bebop artists, who were also composer-performers, were: alto sax player Charlie Parker; tenor sax players Dexter Gordon, Sonny Rollins, and James Moody; trumpeters Fats Navarro, Clifford Brown, and Dizzy Gillespie; pianists Bud Powell, Mary Lou Williams, and Thelonious Monk; electric guitarist Charlie Christian, and drummers Kenny Clarke, Max Roach, and Art Blakey.

The term Bebop came from the nonsense words used by the performers in scat singing. Dizzy Gillespie said that the audiences coined the name after they heard him scat his nameless tunes to his players and the press later picked it up, using it as an official term: "People, when they'd wanna ask for those numbers and didn't know their names, would ask for Bebop. Another theory is that it came from the cry of "Arriba! Arriba!" used by the Latin American bandleaders of the period to encourage their bands.

The path towards streamlined, solo-oriented swing was taken up by bands in the southwest with Kansas City as their musical capital. An ability to play sustained, high energy, creative solos was highly prized for this new style and became the basis of intense competition. The Swing-era jam sessions and "cutting contests" of

Kansas City became legendary. The Kansas approach to swing was epitomised by the Count Basie Orchestra, who came to national prominence in 1937.

One young admirer of the Basie orchestra was a teenage alto saxophone player named Charlie Parker. He was particularly enthralled by their tenor saxophone player Lester Young, who played long flowing melodies that wove through the tune, but somehow always made musical sense.

The overall effect was that his solos became something floating above the music, rather than something springing from it. When Basie's orchestra burst onto the scene in 1937, they gained a national following, with armies of saxophone players striving to imitate Lester Young, drummers wanting to imitate Jo Jones, pianists trying to imitate Basie, and trumpet players striving to imitate Buck Clayton. Parker played along with the new Basie recordings until he could play Young's solos note for note.

As the 30s turned to the 40s, Parker moved to New York as a featured player in the Jay McShann Orchestra. In New York he hooked up with other musicians who were exploring the harmonic and melodic limits of their music, including Dizzy Gillespie. While Gillespie was playing with Cab Calloway, they developed some of the harmonic and chordal innovations that would become the cornerstones of the new music.

Gillespie recorded his first session as a band leader on 9th January 1945, on the Manor label, with Don Byas on tenor, Clyde Hart on Piano, Oscar Pettiford on bass, and Irv Kluger on drums. During the session they recorded "I Can't Get Started", "Good Bait", "Be-Bop (Dizzy's Fingers)", and "Salt Peanuts" (which Manor wrongly called "Salted Peanuts"). Thereafter, Gillespie recorded bebop prolifically and gained recognition as one of its leading figures.

By 1946 bebop had become established as a broad-based movement among Jazz musicians, drawing musicians including trumpeters Fats Navarro and Kenny Dorham, trombonist J. J. Johnson, tenor saxophonists Lucky Thompson, James Moody and Wardell Gray, vibraphonist Milt Jackson, pianists Erroll Garner, Al Haig, and Dodo Marmarosa, bassist Slam Stewart. These and many others contributed to what became known as "Modern Jazz," the favoured music of Britain's early Mods, or Modernists.

Gillespie landed the first recording contract for a major label with their new music, with the RCA Bluebird label recording Dizzy Gillespie and his Orchestra on 22nd February 1946. The tracks were: 52nd Street Theme, A Night in Tunisia, Ol' Man Rebop and Anthropology.

Gillespie, with his extrovert personality and humour, glasses, lip beard and beret, became the most visible symbol of the new Jazz culture and Bebop. His show style, influenced by black vaudeville entertainers, seemed like a throwback to some and also offended some purists ("too much grinning" according to Miles Davis), but it came with a subversive sense of humour that gave a glimpse into an attitude around racial matters, that black musicians had previously avoided. Long before the Civil Rights movement got started, Gillespie confronted the racial divide by lampooning it.

The intellectual subculture that surrounded Bebop turned it into something of a sociological movement as well as a musical one. With the impending demise of the big swing bands, Bebop became the focus of the Jazz world, with a "progressive Jazz" movement seeking to emulate its musical style. Bebop differed immensely from the compositions of the swing era. The music itself sounded very different to the ears of the public, who were used to the bouncy, danceable tunes of Benny Goodman and Glenn Miller. Although it is only part of a rich Jazz tradition, Bebop music continues to be played throughout the world. Trends in improvisation since its era have changed, but the ability to improvise over a complex sequence of altered chords is a fundamental part of any Jazz tuition.

The musical devices developed through Bebop were influential way beyond the Bebop movement itself. "Progressive Jazz" was a broad category of music that included the Bebop-influenced "art music" arrangements used by both the big bands and smaller groups such as those led by Dave Brubeck.

The "Beatnik" look and culture borrowed heavily from the dress and mannerisms of Bebop's musicians and followers, in particular the beret and lip beard of Dizzy Gillespie and the patter and bongo drumming of guitarist Slim Gaillard. The Bebop subculture, defined itself as a non-conformist group expressing its values through musical communion. This would echo in the attitude of the psychedelia-era hippies in the 1960s. Fans of Bebop were not restricted to America; the music also gained cult status in France and Japan.

More recently, Hip Hop artists have cited Bebop as an influence on their rapping style.

Part 4 - The 1950s

Chapter 4.1
The Teds

The 1950s was the decade that gave us the term Teenager and it is generally thought of as the start of youth culture in Britain. While the music of the 50s was very much American, the style and culture was definitely home grown.

If you take any British teenage subculture and trace back its lineage, you will arrive at the same point in time: the Teddy Boys. Long before the Ravers fought with police at illegal parties in the '90s, or Punks were fighting with anyone in the '70s, or the Mods and Rockers clashed violently on Brighton Beach, the Teddy Boys started the very first teenage riot.

When Bill Haley's Rock Around the Clock arrived in England in 1956, the eager Teds erupted: cinema seats were slashed; fireworks and bottles were thrown; shop windows were smashed; and police battled with throngs of singing, jiving, teenagers. Nothing of its sort had been seen before. It caused Britain to wake up in shock at the existence of the teenager, kicking off a moral panic that swept through the media and the middle-aged about 'feral youth' and 'the teen menace'.

The Teddy Boys or Teds were Britain's original teen subculture and they set the template for all of the young tribes that followed in their footsteps: the Mods, Rockers, Punks, New Romantics and beyond. They were inspired by American Rock & Roll and English Edwardian Dandies clothing, which Savile Row tailors had attempted to re-introduce in Britain after the Second World War. The Teds' style was sharp and bold: They wore Brylcreemed quiffs, drainpipe trousers and beetle-crusher shoes.

It is sometimes inaccurately said that the Teddy Boy appeared in Britain during the mid 1950s as a rebellious side effect to the introduction of American Rock & Roll music. But, the Teddy Boy actually predates this and they were a uniquely British phenomenon. The subculture started in London during the early 50s, and quickly spread across Britain, before it became associated with Rock & Roll. Originally known as Cosh Boys, the name Teddy Boy was coined when in 1953, a Daily Express headline shortened Edwardian to Teddy. In 1953, the national newspapers reported on a trend in men's fashion that was sweeping across all of Britain, towards what was termed the New Edwardian look. However, the working class Edwardian style had been worn on the street since at least 1951.

While the clothes were enough to merit little more than a worried glance from the establishment, a number of events quickly conspired to galvanise criticism of the Teds. On the 2nd of July, 1953, a 17-year-old named John Beckley was stabbed to death on Clapham Common by the "Plough Gang", a mob of teenagers who were dressed in "eccentric Edwardian suits".

The *Daily Mirror* headline read: "Flick knives, dance music and

Edwardian suits". That, unsurprisingly, was enough to inflame conservative public opinion; before long, signs appeared at dance halls reading: "No Edwardian clothes or rubber soled footwear."

Although there had previously been youth groups with their own dress codes, like the Scuttlers in 19th century Manchester, Teddy Boys were the first youth group in Britain to identify themselves as teenagers.

In 1956, the movie *Blackboard Jungle* began screening around Britain. It was a tale of American juvenile delinquency, which featured Bill Hayley's "*Rock Around the Clock*" in the opening and closing credits and often triggered riotous behaviour among teenage audiences lapping up the exciting new soundtrack. In London's Elephant and Castle, as well as further afield, gang fights erupted and seats were slashed with razors when ushers told kids to stop dancing in the aisles.

Some Teds formed themselves into gangs and gained notoriety following violent clashes with rival gangs which, like the later fights between Mods and Rockers, were often exaggerated by the press. The most high profile were the 1958 Notting Hill race riots, in which Teddy Boys were present in large numbers and were implicated in several attacks against the West Indian community.

Teddy Boy clothing included drape jackets similar to 1940s American Zoot Suits, usually in dark shades, sometimes with a velvet trim collar and pocket flaps and high-waisted "drainpipe" trousers, often quite short in the leg, exposing the socks. Their outfits also included a high-necked loose-collared white shirt, known as a Mr. B, because it was often worn by Jazz musician Billy Eckstine; a narrow "Slim Jim" tie or western bolo tie, and a fancy brocade waistcoat. Their clothes were mostly tailor-made at great expense, and paid for through weekly instalments.

Favoured footwear included highly polished Oxfords, chunky brogues, and crepe-soled shoes, known as brothel creepers. Their preferred hairstyles included long, strongly-moulded greased-up hair with a quiff at the front and the side combed back to form a duck's arse, or "DA" at the rear.

Teddy Girls too wore drape jackets, with pencil skirts or rolled-up jeans, flat shoes, straw boater hats, cameo brooches, coolie hats and long, elegant clutch bags. Later, they adopted the American fashions of toreador pants, voluminous circle skirts, and wore their hair in ponytails. The Teddy Girls' choice of clothes was not intended just for aesthetic effect; these girls were rejecting post-war austerity. They were young working class women from the poorer districts of London. They typically left school at 14 or 15, to work in factories and offices. Teddy Girls spent much of their free time buying or making their trademark clothes.

Teddy Boys eventually became associated with Rock & Roll music, but prior to the advent of that genre, Teds listened and danced to Jazz and Skiffle music. A well-known dance of the time, that the Teds took to was The Creep, a slow shuffle that became so popular with Teddy Boys that it led to the nickname for their crepe soled shoes, Brothel Creepers. The song "The Creep" was released in 1953 and was written and recorded for HMV by Yorkshire-born big band leader Ken Mackintosh. Although this was not a Rock & Roll record, it was widely adopted by the Teddy Boys of the time. Rock & Roll was only taken up by the Teddy Boys after 1955, when Blackboard Jungle was first shown in cinemas and Teddy Boys started listening to artists like Elvis Presley, Bill Haley and Eddie Cochran.

During the 1970s, Rockabilly music enjoyed renewed popularity and there was a resurgence of interest in Teddy Boy fashion. The look was promoted by Malcolm McLaren and Vivienne Westwood through their shop; Let it Rock, on London's King's Road. The new generation of Teds adopted some aspects of the 50s but added a large glam Rock influence, which included louder colours for drape jackets, brothel creepers and socks and shiny satin shirts worn with bootlace ties, jeans and big-buckled belts. The 1970s Teddy Boys often wore flamboyant pompadour hairstyles with long sideburns and favoured hairspray over grease to style their hair. In the late 70s, the new generation of Teds became enemies of the Sex Pistol-inspired Punk Rockers. In the spring of 1977, street battles between young Punks and older Teds happened on London's King's Road, where the earliest new wave shops, including Westwood and McLaren's Sex; which by now was no longer selling Zoot suits and Ted gear, were located.

This late 70s revival marked my first entry into any form of youth culture in my home town of Mansfield. The Masons Arms, which would later become a biker pub, had regular Rock & Roll Discos. A small cafe, called the Buffet Bar, became a Teddy Boy meeting place, with juke box, pinball and endless cups of tea. We also had several dust ups with Punks from a youth club in nearby Sutton in Ashfield.

Drape Jackets could be bought off the peg in several shops. An ageing Teddy Girl from the first generation, who lived on one of Mansfield's council estates, had a roaring trade in made to measure drape suits. I did not realise it at the time, but the brightly coloured clothes we bought in the 70s were not the original 1950s designs, but the Glam Rock inspired revival style. It was only in researching this book that I saw photographs of the much more stylish darker coloured suits of the 50s.

In the late 1980s, when I had long since moved toward the Rocker subculture, there was a movement to revive the original 1950s Teddy Boy style. In the early 90s, a group of Teddy Boy revivalists in the Tottenham area of north London formed 'The Edwardian Drape Society' (T.E.D.S). The group concentrated on reclaiming the 50s style which they felt had become bastardised by Pop / Glam Rock bands such as Showaddywaddy and Mud in the 70s. T.E.D.S. was the subject of a short film, *The Teddy Boys*, by Bruce Weber.

Nidge, whose real name is John Van Rheede Toas, has been involved with the revival movement since the early 1970s and he remains a passionate advocate for the scene. He is the founder of the encyclopaedic Edwardian Teddy Boy website. In a recent interview, Nidge explained "I can still remember the first time I saw a group of Teds: on Blackpool Promenade, in 1961. I saw these guys who were dressed in drape jackets, the few that remained at that point and also leathers, because the Rockers had started up by then. God knows why, but that image stayed with me," Nidge laughs. "I went to secondary school in 1968, and there were Mods and Rockers at school. Some of the Rockers wore drainpipe jeans with coloured stripes down the side, and quiffs. They just stood out. 1972 was when I got fully into it." "You had the Rockers and the bikers and the Hells Angels, but we got on with them all, for the most part," says Nidge. "A lot of us met in the same pubs. There was always a bit of a mixture between the leather-jacketed Rockers and the Teddy Boys. As the Teddy Boy revival started in the 70s, you'd have Teddy Boys who wore leather jackets during the day and put a drape on at night. The two cultures fused somewhat. The leather jacket was their fighting gear and the drape was the smarter gear you took your missus out in. The Angels liked heavy Rock, but also the Rock & Roll we were into; same with the Rockers."

Just as the Northern Soul scene created eager new ears for impossibly obscure American imports, Rockabilly artists like Don Woody, Sonny Burgess, Ray Campi and Mac Curtis, who were completely unknown over here when they recorded in the 50s, suddenly found eager new listeners. However, while the Soul fans were well catered for on the radio, the BBC did not support the growing interest in Rockabilly and Rock & Roll. It was a situation that led to one of the most energising moments in Ted history, a full scale march to the BBC on the 15th of May 1976 to protest the lack of Rock & Roll radio. "I was in Rhodesia at the time; or else I would have been there. But 6,000 people marched that day," says Nidge. "The BBC played a lot of 60s stuff, but not any Rock & Roll. A 50,000-strong petition and a pilot show were handed in. Out of that march came 'It's Only Rock n Roll', the radio show, and that was an intrinsic part of the culture. "If you were a Ted or a Rocker, you would listen on a Saturday evening w you were getting ready to go out. It was a bit of an underground culture in the 70s, thriving in the pubs and clubs. We'd always supported the underground, the underdog, rather than mainstream artists."

Since the late 70s, the movement has experienced some peaks and troughs. However, in the 90s, two sisters started The Edwardian Drape Society in North London to bring Teds together. The club itself doesn't meet very regularly these days, but they do have regular events under the "Tennessee Club" banner, and throw "The Wildest Cats in Town" weekender, two days of music, dancing and vintage car appreciation, which is attended by Teds, Rockabillys, Rockers and a fair number of what Nidge describes as "weekenders – jive bunnies; they wear the Ted gear to dance in, but don't take the culture any further".

Chapter 4.2
Rock & Roll

Original Rock & Roll, as played by; Eddie Cochran Jerry Lee Lewis and Buddy Holly, had long been part of the Ted's DNA. Rock & Roll began in America during the late 1940s, from black American music styles like gospel, jump blues, Jazz, boogie woogie, and rhythm and blues, along with heavy Country Music influences. While elements of Rock & Roll can be heard in Blues records of the 20s and in country records of the 30s, the genre did not acquire its name until 1954.

In the earliest Rock & Roll styles of the late 40s and early 50s, either the piano or saxophone was usually the lead instrument, but these were replaced or supplemented by guitars in the mid to late 50s. The beat was essentially a blues rhythm with an accentuated backbeat, almost always played on a snare drum. Classic Rock & Roll is usually played with one or two electric guitars (one lead, one rhythm), a double bass or string bass or, after the mid 50s, an electric bass guitar, and a drum kit.

The phrase "Rocking and Rolling" originally described the movement of a ship at sea, but by the early 20th century, it had become used to describe the spiritual fervour of black church rituals and also as a sexual analogy. Many gospel, blues and swing recordings used the phrase in the 40s, on recordings of what became known as "rhythm and blues" music aimed at a black audience.

By 1943, the Rock & Roll Inn in New Jersey was established as a music venue. Then in 1951, disc jockey Alan Freed began playing this music style whilst popularising the phrase to describe it.

The origins of Rock & Roll have been fiercely debated by music historians. There is a general agreement that it arose in the Southern States, a region which produced most of the big, early Rock & Roll acts, through merging African musical traditions with European instrumentation. The migration of former slaves and their descendants to urban centres such as St. Louis, Memphis, New York City, Detroit, Chicago, Cleveland, and Buffalo meant that black and white people were living closely together in larger numbers than ever before and as a result heard each other's music and began to copy each other's fashions.

In the 1930s, Jazz, and Swing, from urban-based dance bands and blues influenced country swing, were among the first music to present black American sounds for a predominantly white audience. One noteworthy example of a Jazz song with recognisable Rock & Roll elements was Big Joe Turner and pianist Pete Johnson's 1939 single *Roll 'Em Pete*, which is regarded as an important precursor to Rock & Roll.

In the 40s, particularly on the West Coast and Midwest, the development of jump blues, with its guitar riffs, prominent beats and shouted lyrics, set the stage for later developments in Rock & Roll. In the documentary film *Hail! Hail! Rock & Roll*, Keith Richards suggested that Chuck Berry developed his brand of Rock & Roll, by transposing the familiar two-note lead line of jump blues piano directly to the electric guitar, creating what is now instantly recognisable as Rock guitar. Similarly, country boogie and Chicago electric blues supplied many of the elements that would be thought of as characteristically Rock & Roll. Inspired by electric blues, Chuck Berry introduced his aggressive guitar sound to Rock & Roll and established the electric guitar as its centrepiece.

Rock & Roll arrived at a time of considerable technological change in the music business, soon after the development of the electric guitar, amplifier and microphone, and the 45 rpm record. There were also changes in the record industry, with the rise of independent labels like Atlantic, Sun and Chess servicing niche audiences and a similar rise in the popularity of radio stations that played their music. It was the realisation that relatively affluent white teenagers were listening to this music that led to the development of Rock & Roll as a distinct genre.

In July 1954, Elvis Presley recorded *That's All Right* at Sam Phillips' Sun Studio in Memphis. Three months earlier, on 12th April 1954, Bill Haley & the Comets recorded *Rock Around the Clock*. It was only a minor hit when first released, but when it accompanied the opening sequence of Blackboard Jungle a year later, it set the Rock & Roll boom in motion. The song became one of the biggest hits of all time and frenzied teens flocked to see Haley and the Comets perform it, causing riots in some cities. *Rock Around the Clock* was a breakthrough for both the group and for Rock & Roll music in general. If everything that came before laid the groundwork, *Rock*

Around the Clock brought Rock & Roll to a global audience.

Rockabilly, with its county music roots, was the style I favoured in the 70s and it still lives on in the biker culture today, with many bike rallies featuring Rockabilly bands. The centre piece of today's Rockabilly Bands is usually a brightly painted Double Bass, plucked, rather than bowed. The bass player's party piece is often to climb on his instrument while playing it. At one North East bike rally, I watched a particularly talented bassist playing *Duelling Banjos*, while perched on top of his Double Bass.

The term Rockabilly usually refers to the type of Rock & Roll music that was played and recorded in the mid 50s, mostly by white singers such as Elvis Presley, Carl Perkins, Johnny Cash, and Jerry Lee Lewis.

Many other popular Rock & Roll singers of the time, like Fats Domino and Little Richard, came out of the black rhythm and blues tradition and are not usually classed as Rockabilly.

In 1956, the arrival of Rockabilly was underlined by the success of songs like *Folsom Prison Blues* by Johnny Cash, *Blue Suede Shoes* by Carl Perkins and *Heartbreak Hotel* by Elvis. For a few years it was the most commercially successful form of Rock & Roll. Later Rockabilly acts, particularly performing songwriters like Buddy Holly, would have a major influence on British acts, including the song writing of the Beatles and through them on the style of later Rock music.

Many of the earliest white Rock & Roll hits were covers or partial re-writes of earlier black Rhythm and Blues or Blues songs. Through the late 40s and early 50s, Rhythm and Blues music gained a stronger beat and a wilder style, with artists like Fats Domino and Johnny Otis speeding up the tempo and increasing the backbeat. Before the efforts of Freed and other DJs, black music was taboo on many white owned radio stations, but artists and producers quickly recognised the potential of Rock & Roll. Most of Elvis Presley's early hits were covers of black Rhythm and Blues or Blues songs, like *That's All Right*, a countrified arrangement of an earlier blues number, *Baby Let's Play House, Lawdy Miss Clawdy* and *Hound Dog*.

In the late 50s and early 60s Rock n Roll went through something of a bad patch when, in 1959 Buddy Holly, The Big Bopper and Ritchie Valens died together in a plane crash and Elvis was called up for military service in Germany. This was on top of the retirement of Little Richard to become a preacher in 1957, the scandal surrounding Jerry Lee Lewis' marriage to his thirteen year old cousin in 1958, the arrest of Chuck Berry in 1959 and the Payola scandal which implicated major industry figures, including Alan Freed, in taking bribes to promote individual acts or songs.

As recording technology improved, there were several innovative developments that built on Rock & Roll's rough beginnings, including multitrack recording, developed by Les Paul, the electronic treatment of sound by such innovators as *Telstar* producer Joe Meek and Phil Spector's Wall of Sound productions, which used a full orchestra behind his artists. These innovations led to differing genres of music, like the rise of surf music, garage Rock and the Twist dance craze. Surf Rock in particular, with its use of reverb guitars, became one of the most popular forms of American Rock in the 60s.

Britain in the 1950s was well placed to receive American Rock & Roll music. We share a common language, had been exposed to American culture through the stationing of troops in Britain and shared many social developments, including the emergence of distinct youth subcultures, which in Britain included the Teddy Boys. Trad Jazz became popular, and many of its artists were influenced by American styles, including Boogie Woogie and the Blues. The Skiffle craze, led by Lonnie Donegan, utilised amateurish versions of American folk songs and encouraged many of the next generation of Rock & Roll musicians to start performing.

The initial response of the British music industry was to try and produce copies of American records, recorded with session musicians and often fronted by teen idols, like Wee Willie Harris and Tommy Steele. In 1958 Britain produced its first "authentic" Rock & Roll song when Cliff Richard reached number two in the charts with *Move It*. At the same time, TV shows like *Six-Five Special* and Oh Boy! boosted the careers of British Rock & Rollers like Marty Wilde and Adam Faith. Cliff Richard and his backing band, the Shadows, were the most successful home grown Rock & Roll act of the era. Other prominent acts included Billy Fury, Joe Brown, and Johnny Kidd & the Pirates, whose 1960 hit song "*Shakin' All Over*" became a Rock & Roll standard, covered by Motorhead in 1980, collaborating with Girl School, under the name Head Girl.

Interest in Rock & Roll was beginning to subside in America by the early 60s, but it was taken up by groups in British cities like Liverpool, Manchester, Birmingham, and London. Many groups moved towards the beat music of Rock & Roll and Rhythm and Blues from Skiffle, like the Quarrymen who became the Beatles.

The British revival gained international success from 1964 onwards, with what became known in America as the British Invasion. Groups that followed after the Beatles included Freddie and the Dreamers, Wayne Fontana and the Mindbenders, Herman's Hermits and the Dave Clark Five. Early British Rhythm and Blues groups with more of a Blues influence included the Animals, the Yardbirds and the Rolling Stones, who went onto superstardom.

Chapter 4.3
The Rockers

Today's Teddy Boy revivalists favour big classic cars from the 50s, such as the Ford Zodiac. But for the youngsters of the 1950s, cars were much too expensive to be within their reach. For the working class Teds of Britain, motorcycles were their only available transport. The practicalities of dressing to ride a motorcycle prompted a move away from their smart, Edwardian drape jackets, towards leather jackets and denim jeans. Rockers, leather boys and Ton-up boys are all names given to a biker subculture centred on British café racers and Rock & Roll music. By 1965, the term greaser had also been added. This is the subculture that has remained closest to my heart. As a teenager, I enjoyed a brief dalliance with the 1970s Teddy Boy revival, before a love of motorcycles made leather and denim more practical.

Motorcycle clubs are still prevalent today, with a generally older age group than in the 50s. For the most part, there has been a move towards Heavy Rock by the bikers, but there remain many bikers who favour Rockabilly and many who style themselves on the Ted inspired Rockers

There were many factors that conspired to kick start the British Rocker subculture like: the end of post-war rationing, a rise in the prosperity of working class youths, the availability of credit to young people, the building of race track-like arterial roads around our cities, the development of transport cafes and a high point for British motorcycle engineering. During the 50s, the Rockers were known as "Ton-Up boys" because "doing a ton" is slang for riding at speeds of 100 mph or more. The image of the Rockers, with their slicked back hair and side burns came from the Teddy boys, who are considered their "spiritual ancestors"

From the 1960s onwards, due to the media fury surrounding the Mods and Rockers, motorcycling youths became more commonly known as Rockers. The public came to think of Rockers as loutish, scruffy outsiders.
Rockers wore heavily decorated leather bike jackets, adorned with metal studs, patches and pin badges. When they rode their bikes, they wore an open face helmet, flying goggles and a white silk scarf to protect them from the elements. Largely because of their clothing styles and dirtiness, Rockers were not widely welcomed in the dance halls. Rockers also transformed Rock & Roll dancing into a more violent, individualistic form beyond the control of dance hall management.

The media created animosity between the Mods and the Rockers. The Mods or Modernists, as they were known were a youth subculture that liked stylish clothes and Scooters and were regarded as being the smarter dressed of the two groups. The Rockers and the Mods got along ok at a distance. The Mods were into pill popping with purple hearts and bennies being their favourites, whereas the Rockers liked beer and cigarettes and were mostly anti drugs.

During the summer both groups migrated towards the seaside, particularly Brighton, Margate and Ramsgate. Many people felt uneasy with the large groups wandering the streets calling each other names. The Rockers called the Mods "children" because they rode prams and they called the bikers "greebos" as they wore brylcream in their hair or had greasy hair due to the sweat from their helmets.

On the Whitsuntide weekend of May 1964, the youths of Britain went mad, if you believed the papers, that is. Whitsun 1964 became famous as the peak of the Mods and Rockers riots, when large groups of teenagers caused mayhem in southern resort towns. Extensively photographed and publicised at the time, these disturbances entered popular folklore. Yet, when you deal with tabloid newspapers, things are not always as they are published. What was painted as an example of national degeneration was to some extent, hyped up by the press. It was nothing like as bad as the headlines suggested. Although an estimated 1,000 youths were present during the Brighton disturbances, there were only 76 arrests. In Margate, there were about 400 youths involved, with only 64 arrests. While unpleasant, this was hardly a teen take-over.

The build up began six weeks earlier, during a cold Easter weekend. 1,000 or so young Londoners travelled to Clacton, on the south east coast. Bored with the bad weather and limited facilities, groups separated according to their individual tribes: there were scuffles and stone-throwing and a generally threatening appearance of the teenagers en masse, barely controlled by an underwhelming police presence.

On Easter Monday, the press went big with the story, 'Day of Terror by Scooter Groups' (*Daily Telegraph*), 'Youngsters Beat Up Town - 97 Leather Jacket Arrests' (*Daily Express*), and 'Wild Ones Invade Seaside - 97 Arrests' (*Daily Mirror*). The stories described: "fighting, drinking, roaring, rampaging teenagers on scooters and motorcycles".

By the early 70s, the British Rocker and hardcore biker scene fractured and evolved under the new influences from California: the Hippies and the Hells Angels. The remaining Rockers became known as greasers and the scene began to die out. Despite the influence of the big American clubs, pockets of bikers loyal to the British Rocker image did carry on. My very first bike club experience in the early 80s was with The Rebel Riders; very much a Rockabilly orientated Motorcycle Club.

London's Ace Cafe is still the centre point for what remains of the Rocker scene, its owners were even canny enough to Trademark the Rockers name. The Ace is a former transport cafe on London's North Circular Road, It is historically notable as a venue in motorcycling culture which originally operated from 1938 until 1969, before re-opening on the original site in 1997. The Ace Cafe opened its doors in 1938 to cater for traffic on the new North Circular Road. Because the cafe was open 24 hours a day, it began to attract bikers, becoming popular with the Ton Up Boys in the 50s and the Rockers in the 60s.
The Ace still hosts regular Rockers Reunions for the many Cafe

Racer and British bike enthusiasts who are still around.

The Rockers, their origins and the continuation of their subculture is covered in greater detail in my book Mofos: a history of British Biker culture.

Chapter 4.4
The Beatniks

In late 1940s America, a trend developed among young college students to adopt the trademark image of bebop trumpeter Dizzy Gillespie by wearing goatees, horn-rimmed glasses, and berets, rolling their own cigarettes and playing bongos.

What was for Gillespie, just an eccentric stage image, became to the students a badge of bohemian pseudo-intellectualism.

Fashions for women included black leotards with their hair worn; long, straight and unadorned in a rebellion against the middle class culture of beauty salons.

As one might expect of pre-smartphone students, they were quite a literary bunch and adopted as a manifesto Jack Kerouac's autobiographical novels. Kerouac introduced the phrase "Beat Generation" in 1948, generalising from his own social circle to characterise the underground, anti-conformist youth in New York at the time.

They became known as Beatniks, although this was a media stereotype coined by Herb Caen in his 1958 article in the *San Francisco Chronicle*. Caen created the word by adding the Russian suffix -nik to the name "Beat Generation" that Kerouac had introduced. Caen's article with the word came just six months after the launch of Russian satellite Sputnik.

The adjective "beat" came from underworld slang; the world of hustlers, drug addicts, and petty thieves, from where Kerouac sought his inspiration. "Beat" was slang for "beaten down" or downtrodden. But Kerouac gave it a spiritual meaning as in "beatitude," the proverb-like proclamations told by Jesus in his Sermon on the Mount.

Kerouac's vision for the Beat Generation, in the late Forties, was of a generation of illuminated hipsters hitchhiking around America, ragged, beatific and beautiful in an ugly, but graceful new way. His was a vision gleaned from the way he had heard the word "beat" used on street corners around Times Square ; beat, meaning down and out but full of intense conviction. He had heard old 1910 Daddy Hipsters speak the word that way. It never meant juvenile delinquents, it meant characters of a special spirituality who didn't gang up but were solitary figures.

Kerouac explained what he meant by "beat" at a forum called, "Is There A Beat Generation?" on 8th November 1958, at New York's Hunter College Playhouse. The other Panellists at the seminar all wore suits, while Kerouac wore black jeans, ankle boots and a checked shirt. Reading from a prepared text, Kerouac reflected on his own beat beginnings: "It is because I am Beat, that is, I believe in beatitude and that god so loved the world that he gave his only begotten son to it... Who knows, but that the universe is not one vast sea of compassion actually, the veritable holy honey, beneath all this show of personality and cruelty?"

Possibly the first movie portrayal of the Beat society was in 1949 film *D.O.A.* In the film the main character goes to a loud San Francisco bar, where a woman shouts to the musicians: "Cool! Cool!

Really Cool!" One of the characters says, "Man, am I really hip", and another replies, "You're from nowhere, nowhere!" Typical 1940s attire was mixed with Beatnik clothing styles, particularly in one male who had a Beatnik hat, long hair, and a moustache with goatee, but still wore a dress suit. The bartender referred to one of his patrons as "Jive Crazy" and talks about the music driving its followers crazy. He then told one man to "Calm down Jack!" and the man replied, "Oh don't bother me, man. I'm being enlightened!" The cartoon depictions are probably more memorable to my generation. Hanna Barbera's series *Top Cat* featured a Beatnik cat named Spook and *Scooby-Doo*, featured the Beatnik character Shaggy.

Like the youth cultures that would follow, the Beatnik image became a product to be marketed. The stereotype was soon absorbed into American culture: the idea of the "Beat Generation" sold books, black turtleneck sweaters and bongos, berets and dark glasses. It sold a way of life that seemed like dangerous fun, to be either condemned or imitated. Suburban couples had Beatnik parties on Saturday nights, drank too much and fondled each other's wives. What came out in the media, in; newspapers, magazines, TV and the movies, was a product of stereotypes created in the 30s and 40s. It was a garbled mix of 1920s Greenwich Village bohemian artist and Bebop musicians, whose visual image was completed by mixing a beret, a Vandyck beard, a turtleneck sweater, a pair of sandals, and a set of bongo drums. A few authentic elements were added to the image: for example, poets reading their poems, but even this was made unintelligible by portraying the poets speaking in a phoney Bebop idiom.

The Beat philosophy was mostly countercultural and anti-materialistic and stressed the importance of improving one's inner self over and above material possessions. Some Beat writers, like Alan Watts, began to delve into Eastern religions such as Buddhism and Taoism. Their politics tended to be liberal, left-wing and anti-war. The Beatnik movement introduced Asian religions to Western society. These religions had a significant impact on the Beat generation because they provided the movement with new views on the world. By 1958, many beat writers published writings focusing on Buddhism. 1958 was also the year Jack Kerouac published his novel *The Dharma Bums*. Kerouac discovered an interest in Buddhism following the many traumatic events that occurred in his lifetime. His fascination focused on the Four Noble Truths established by Buddha.

Allen Ginsberg's spiritual journey to India in 1963 also influenced the Beat movement. This voyage brought him enlightenment regarding Asian religions, because he studied religious texts alongside the monks. The poet deduced that what linked the function of poetry to Asian religions was their mutual goal towards achieving ultimate truth. His Discovery of Hindu mantra chants subsequently influenced Beat poetry. What the many Beat pioneers, who followed a spiritual Buddhist path, appreciated about Asian religions was their profound understanding of human nature and insights into the being, existence and reality of mankind.

Beat authors borrowed heavily from the Jazz / Hipster slang of the 40s, peppering their works with words such as "square", "cats", "cool", and "dig", but Jazz was much more than just a vocabulary to the Beat writers. To them, Jazz was a way of life, a completely different and improvisational way to approach the creative process. The need for teenagers to have their own language, unintelligible to adults has been a continuing theme over the decades. Today; "sick" is substituted for good, your friends are "bro" or "bruv," sentences are routinely ended with "init." Possibly the funniest example I heard was in 2017, at the Police Custody Desk, where a young man who had been on the run phoned his mum. The first words out of his mouth were "Po Po got me init."

Since 1958, the terms Beat Generation and Beat have both been used to describe the anti-materialistic literary movement that began with Kerouac in the 40s, stretching through into the 60s. The Beat philosophy of anti-materialism and soul searching influenced 1960s musicians like Bob Dylan, the early Pink Floyd, and The Beatles. However, the soundtrack to the Beat movement was the Modern Jazz pioneered by saxophonist Charlie Parker and trumpeter Dizzy Gillespie, that the media called Bebop.

Musically the 'Beat' influence was extensive and even the Beatles used the word beat in their name. Ray Manzarek of the Doors was quoted saying that they wanted to be Beatniks and Jim Morrison was heavily influenced by Jack Kerouac. Allen Ginsberg's

Christmas card list read like a who's-who of 1960s cool, due to him being friends with Paul McCartney, Bob Dylan, the Rolling Stones, Lou Reed and the Grateful Dead to name but a few.

By 1960, a small "Beatnik" group in Newquay, Cornwall attracted the attention and the abhorrence of their neighbours for growing their hair to a length past the shoulders, resulting in a television interview with Alan Whicker on BBC television's Tonight series.

As was the way back then, trends and fashions moved very quickly and 1967 became a watershed year for both fashion and musical terms. January 1967 saw the "Human Be-In" at the Golden Gate Park in San Francisco, which was essentially a protest against a California law banning LSD. It was where Timothy Leary first used the term 'turn on, tune in, drop out'. This event is viewed by many as being the first Hippie gathering. The Summer of Love that followed saw the Hippie revolution spread from the west coast of America to Europe and the rest of the World. In no time at all there was free love everywhere, tie-dyed t-shirts and huge flairs. Any self-respecting Beatnik could not ignore this overwhelming new fashion and in no time at all the psychedelic revolution took over. It is interesting to note that the name Hippie derives from the word Hipster, which was what a lot of the early Beatniks were called. Hipster also gained a renaissance in the 21st century, with beards, check shirts and anything retro coming back into fashion.

It can be argued that the progression from Beatnik to Hippie was a natural one, almost evolutionary in its manner. The Beatnik's drug of choice; marijuana was enhanced with LSD and their dark sombre clothes were replaced with the Hippies bright colourful kaftans. Musically the Beatles release of '*Sgt Pepper's Lonely Hearts Club Band*' in June 1967 couldn't have come at a better time and proved to be a game changer. It was a perfect storm of music and events coming together to have a massive influence around the World. Beatniks didn't so much die out as morph into hippies.

Part 5 - The 1960s

Chapter 5.1
The Mods

The Mod subculture has its roots in a small group of stylish Londoners in the late 50s who were called modernists because they listened to Modern Jazz, as opposed to Traditional Jazz. The main elements of their subculture included: fashion, often including tailor-made suits; music, including Soul, Ska, and R&B; scooters and amphetamine fuelled all night dancing.

During the 1960s, some Mods became embroiled in well publicised fights with the Rockers, who considered the Mods to be effeminate, because of their interest in fashion. But by 1965, these conflicts had begun to subside and Mods increasingly gravitated towards Pop Art and Psychedelia.

Some people say that the Mod culture had its roots in the 1950s Beatnik coffee bar culture of art school students in London's radical Bohemian scene. Some of the original Mods agree that it was began as an extension of the Beatnik culture, stressing that it came from 'Modernist' as it was to do with Modern Jazz. They now say Mod has become misunderstood as purely a working-class, scooter-riding precursor to the Skinheads.

Coffee bars became attractive to British youths, including Mods and Rockers, because, unlike pubs, which closed at about 11pm, they were open until the early hours of the morning. Coffee bars had jukeboxes, which sometimes had reserved space in the machines for the customers' own records.

Due to the increased affluence of post-war Britain, the youths in the early 60s were one of the first generations that did not have to contribute their money from after-school jobs to the family finances. When Mod teens began using their disposable income to buy stylish clothes, the first youth-targeted boutiques opened in the Carnaby Street and King's Road districts of London.

Male Mods adopted a smooth look that included suits with narrow lapels, thin ties, button-down collar shirts, wool or cashmere jumpers and hairstyles which imitated French Nouvelle Vague film actors. A few male Mods went against gender norms by wearing eye shadow, eye-pencil and even lipstick.

Mods chose scooters over motorbikes partly because they symbolised Italian style and partly because their body panels made them less likely to stain clothes with oil or road dust. Many Mods wore military parkas while riding scooters in order to keep their clothes clean. Others wore Yogi Coats'. These were not parkas like the Mods are normally pictured wearing. They were a woollen coat with long strands, a bit like an Astrakhan coat and were usually US Army surplus. Yogi Coats pre dated parkas for wearing on the scooter.

There were always trend setters, among the Mods. These were always the first to wear a new fashion, with the others quickly following their lead. These lead figures became known as "Faces." Sting's character in the Who's *Quadrophenia* was called The Ace Face, indicating that he was way ahead of the trends. Unlike the rest of his group, Sting stood out by riding his scooter in a grey leather trench coat, rather than the ubiquitous parka.

Quadrophenia was a 1979 film, based on The Who's 1973 Rock opera. Its unusual title is not based on anything Mod related, it refers to the four acts of the Rock Opera LP record. The film stars Phil Daniels as Jimmy, a young 1960s Mod who escaped from his dead-end job as a mailroom boy by dancing, taking amphetamines, riding his scooter, and brawling with the Rockers. After he and his friends had a huge brawl with the Rockers at Brighton, he was arrested and discovered that his idol, the "Ace Face" was actually a Bell Boy at a hotel. This finale to the film emphasised that most of the youth cultures developed as an escape from very mundane lives.

Female Mods dressed androgynously, with short haircuts, men's trousers and shirts, flat shoes, and very little makeup; often just pale foundation, brown eye shadow, pale lipstick and false eyelashes. As female Mod fashion became more mainstream, slender models like Jean Shrimpton and Twiggy began to exemplify the Mod look. Mod fashion designers emerged, such as Mary Quant, who became known for her miniskirt designs, which became progressively shorter throughout the 60s.

Newspaper accounts usually focused on the Mod obsession with clothes, often detailing prices of their expensive suits and seeking out extreme cases such as a young Mod who claimed that he would "go without food to buy clothes".

Two previous youth subcultures helped pave the way for Mod fashion by breaking new ground; the Beatniks, with their Bohemian image of berets and black turtlenecks and the Teddy Boys, from whom the Mods inherited their fastidious fashion tendencies and their immaculate dandy look. The Teddy Boys paved the way for male interest in fashion becoming socially acceptable, because prior to the Teddy Boys, male interest in fashion was mostly associated with the flamboyant style of the underground homosexual culture.

The influence of British newspapers in crafting a public perception of Mods as having a leisure filled club-going lifestyle can be seen in a 1964 article in the Sunday Times. The paper interviewed a 17 year old mod who went clubbing seven nights a week and spent his Saturday afternoons shopping for clothes and records. However, this was a long way from describing a typical Mod, as very few British teens or young adults would have had the time and money to spend going to nightclubs. Most Mods worked 9 to 5 in semi-skilled jobs, which meant that they had much less leisure time and a modest income to spend.

A big part of the Mod subculture was amphetamine use, which they used to fuel all-night dances at clubs like Manchester's Twisted Wheel. Newspaper reports described dancers leaving clubs at 5 a.m. with dilated pupils, something that would be replicated in the Northern Soul and Rave scenes of later generations. They favoured a combined amphetamine / barbiturate called Drinamyl, nicknamed "purple hearts," which were still legal during the early 60s.

Mods used the drug for stimulation and alertness, which they thought different from the intoxication caused by alcohol and other drugs. To them, amphetamines symbolised a smart, on-the-ball, cool image that gave them stimulation and greater awareness, rather than the drunken rowdiness of the Rockers.

Commentators argue that the significance of amphetamines in the Mod culture was similar to that of LSD and cannabis to the later Hippie counterculture. Mods used amphetamines to extend their leisure time into the early hours of the morning. But drugs also provided a way of bridging the gap between their drudging everyday work lives and their "inner world" of dancing and dressing up.

Mods also treated their scooters as a fashion accessory. Italian scooters were preferred due to their clean, curving shapes and gleaming chrome. For Mods, Italian scooters were the embodiment of continental style and provided a way of escaping the working class houses of their upbringing. Mods customised their scooters by painting them in two-tone and candy flake and by over accessorising them with luggage racks, crash bars and lots of mirrors. Some Mods added as many as 30 mirrors to their scooters. This fashion started when a law was passed demanding "at least one" mirror on motorcycles. They sometimes took their engine side panels and front bumpers to electroplating shops and had them plated in chrome.

The early Mods listened to the sophisticated smooth Modern Jazz of musicians like Miles Davis, Charlie Parker, Dave Brubeck and the Modern Jazz Quartet, as well as American rhythm and blues artists such as Bo Diddley and Muddy Waters. Black American servicemen, stationed in Britain during the early part of the Cold War, brought over records that were not available in Britain and they sold these to young Londoners. Starting around 1960, Mods began to embrace the off-beat, Jamaican Ska music of artists such as the Skatalites, Owen Gray, Derrick Morgan and Prince Buster.
The original Mods gathered at all-night clubs such as The Flamingo and The Marquee in London to hear the latest records and show off their dance moves. As the Mod subculture spread across Britain, other clubs became popular, including the Twisted Wheel Club in Manchester.

British bands like The Rolling Stones, Yardbirds and The Kinks all had a Mod following and other bands started to emerge that were specifically Mod oriented. These included The Who, Small Faces, the Creation, The Action, The Smoke and John's Children. The Who's early promotional material portrayed them as playing "maximum rhythm and blues." Although The Beatles dressed like Mods for a while, their beat music was not as popular as R&B among Mods.

When Mod became more cosmopolitan during the "Swinging London" period, some working class "Street Mods" splintered off; forming other groups such Rude Boys and what would eventually become known as Skinheads.

By 1963, the Mods had gradually accumulated the identifying symbols with which they are now associated, such as scooters, amphetamine pills and R&B music. While clothes remained important, they could now be off the peg.

Hard Mods, who later evolved into Skinheads, rode scooters for more practical reasons. Their scooters were either unmodified or cut down, which were nicknamed "skelly". Lambrettas were cut down to the bare frame and Vespas, with their monocoque design, had their body panels slimmed down or reshaped.

In more recent times, Lambrettas have attracted an eclectic following of "revival" Mods and other scooterists. Vespa and Lambrettas both can be converted to relatively fast machines with a little, relatively expensive, modification. Many owners customised their scooters with elaborate paintwork and showed them off at scooter rallies.

There was a Mod revival in England in the late 1970s, which attempted to replicate the "scooter" period look and styles of the early- to mid- 1960s. A Mod revival started in the late 70s, with thousands of Mod revivalists attending scooter rallies in places like Scarborough and the Isle of Wight. This revival was partly inspired by the Who's 1979 film *Quadrophenia*.

There are still many clubs across the world, both nationaly and locally, devoted to Lambretta and Vespa scooters. The clubs still organise ride outs and rallies which take place during weekends throughout the summer months and have high attendance. Some rallies achieve 2,500 paying rally goers.

Chapter 5.2
Football Hooligans.

Of all the gang related cultures our country has seen, one stands out as by far the most tribal of them all. Football hooliganism seems to harken back to our most primal instincts as pack animals. The subculture is slightly out of kilter with others featured in this book, because, in common with the Scuttlers, it is not linked to any particular musical genre. The actual football seems secondary to the violence, as often the gangs never even enter a football ground. The gangs often call themselves Football Firms, the term coming from London slang for a criminal gang. They are come together specifically to intimidate and attack supporters of other teams. Other names commonly used to describe hooligan firms include "army", "boys", "casuals", and "crew". The term "Casuals" was coined in the late 70s and has become one of the most often used names for the hooligan groups.

Certain clubs have long-running rivalries with other clubs and hooliganism associated with matches between them, called local derbies, is likely to be quite severe. Where I live and work, there are two key problem derbies, known to the police as Cat A matches. These are: Mansfield v Chesterfield (known as "Spireites" because of the town's Crooked Spire) and Nottingham Forest v Derby County.
Nottingham Forest has two groups of hooligans; an older, more experienced group known as The Executive Crew and a younger,

up and coming group called the Forest Nasty Squad. A calling card I seized from a young Nasty Squad member read; "We are Forest, we are nasty, you've just met the squad."

Conflict can take place before, during or after matches. Hooligans usually select locations away from the ground to avoid arrest, but fights can also erupt spontaneously inside the ground, or in the surrounding streets.

 Hooligan-led violence is sometimes called "aggro," short for "aggravation" and "bovver," from the Cockney pronunciation of "bother."

I chose to place this section within the 1960s, as that is when football hooliganism first became widely publicised, but it started much earlier and continues to the present day. As a youth culture, it has outlasted all the rest.

The phenomenon of football violence can be traced back to 14th century England. In 1314, Edward II banned football; which was at that time, a violent and unruly activity involving rival villages kicking a pig's bladder across the local heath. The King believed the disorder surrounding matches might lead to social unrest, or even treason.

According to a University of Liverpool academic paper, conflict at an 1846 match in Derby, needed a reading of the "Riot Act" and two squads of Dragoons to effectively deal with the disorderly crowd. This same paper also identified "pitch invasions" as a common occurrence during the 1880s.

The first recorded examples of football hooliganism in the modern game occurred during the 1880s, a period when gangs of fans would intimidate entire neighbourhoods, as well as attacking referees, opposing supporters and players. In 1885, after Preston North End beat Aston Villa 5–0 in a friendly game, both teams were pelted with stones, hit with sticks, punched, kicked and spat at. One Preston player was beaten so badly that he lost consciousness. Press reports of the time described the fans as "howling roughs". The following year, Preston fans fought Queen's Park Rangers fans in a railway station; the first known instance of football hooliganism outside of a match. In 1905, several Preston fans were tried for hooliganism, including a "drunk and disorderly" 70 year old woman, after their game against Blackburn Rovers.

Football crowd violence has been a feature of Association Football throughout its history. Millwall's ground was closed in 1920, 1934 and 1950 following crowd disturbances, cementing the club's current reputation for violence. But the phenomenon only began to gain media attention in the late 50s due to the emergence of extreme violence in South American football.

In the 1955–56 English football season, Liverpool and Everton supporters were involved in several incidents and, by the 60s, an average of 25 hooligan incidents were reported each year. The label "football hooliganism" first appeared in the media during the mid-60s, leading to increased media interest in, and reporting of, acts of disorder. Just as happened with the Teds, Mods and a Rockers, it has been said that the media fuelled a moral panic out of proportion to the scale of the actual problem.

Football hooliganism has factors in common with juvenile delinquency and what academics call "ritualised male violence." Sports Studies scholars at Liverpool Hope University said in a 2008 study that "Involvement in football violence can be explained in relation to a number of factors, relating to interaction, identity, legitimacy and power." Football violence is also said to reflect strong emotional ties to a football team, which may help reinforce a supporter's sense of identity." This sense of identity has been seen many times before and since, in the various gang cultures' attention to their dress code.

Football hooligans often appear to be less interested in the football match than its associated violence. There behaviour risks them being arrested before the match, denied admittance to the stadium, ejected during the match or banned from attending future matches. Hooligan groups often associate themselves with, and congregate in, a specific "end" of their team's stadium, and sometimes they include the section's name in the name of their group. Notts County's hooligan element calls themselves "The Roadside Casuals," in reference to their stand being alongside the road.

In the 60s and early 70s football hooliganism was associated with the Skinheads. Later, the Casual subculture transformed the British hooligan scene. Instead of wearing working class Skinhead style clothes, which easily identified hooligans to the police, hooligans began wearing designer clothes and expensive sportswear, particularly Stone Island, Burberry, Prada, Sergio Tacchini and Adidas.

By the 60s England had a worldwide reputation for football violence; the phenomenon was often called the English Disease. From the 70s, lots of organised hooligan firms sprang up, with most Football League clubs having at least one organised hooligan element. Hooliganism was often at its worst when local rivals played each other. Supporters of teams including Arsenal, Leeds United, Chelsea, Millwall, Tottenham Hotspur, Portsmouth, West Ham, Leicester and Bristol City were among those most frequently linked with hooliganism.

Racism became a big factor in hooliganism around the same time, as black players became more common in English league teams in the 70s. Black players were often targeted with monkey chants, or had bananas thrown at them. Members of far-right groups like the National Front also sprayed racist slogans and distributed racist literature at matches.

Sectarian violence between Catholic and Protestant fans has long been a regular cause of crowd violence and offensive chanting, at matches in Scotland between Celtic and Rangers and in Liverpool, between Everton and Liverpool.

As a result of the 1985 Heysel Stadium disaster in Brussels, where Liverpool fans rioting led to the deaths of 39 Juventus fans, English clubs were banned from all European competition until 1990, with Liverpool banned for a further year.

English clubs who made the headlines for the worst examples of hooliganism include Birmingham City, whose multi racial hooligan element were called "Zulus" by fans of rival teams in the 70s when football hooligans were almost always white British. Chelsea chairman Ken Bates installed an electric fence at his club's stadium in the mid 80s to combat hooligans, but was refused permission to switch it on during matches. The Chelsea's Head-hunters hooligan element was subject of a very disturbing undercover TV documentary. Leeds United were banned from European competitions after a riot at the 1975 European Cup final against Bayern München. Liverpool became notorious for the deaths at Heysel Stadium. Manchester United were kicked out of the European Cup Winner's Cup in 1977 after their fans rioted during a game in France. Millwall's most notorious hooliganism incident was in 1985 when their fans rioted in an FA Cup tie at Luton. Tottenham Hotspur had a group of fans banned from all football grounds in England in 2008 for racial and homophobic abuse towards former player Sol Campbell.

Football hooliganism has been portrayed in films such as *ID, The Firm, Cass, The Football Factory, Green Street, Rise of the Footsoldier, Awaydays* and *The Brothers Grimsby*. There are also many books featuring hooliganism, such as *The Football Factory* and *Among the Thugs*. Some critics argue that these media representations glamorise violence and the hooligan lifestyle.

As with the other subcultures looking for a sense of identity, the football hooligans have always sought a distinctive look. Initially, it was hats and scarves knitted in the club's colours. Even haircuts were used to display identity; as a bouncer in 1980's Mansfield, I would refuse entry to anyone with a "Carrot Top" haircut. This odd cut, shaved at the sides and sticking up at the top, was the trademark of Mansfield Town's Carrot Crew hooligan firm.

The Casual subculture developed as a defence against the police being able to identify them. Instead of coloured football clothing or distinctive hair cuts, the hooligans took to wearing expensive designer clothing, known as "clobber." The subculture originated in the early 80s when hooligans began wearing designer clothing and expensive sportswear in order to avoid the attention of police and to intimidate their rivals. They did not wear club colours, so it was easier to infiltrate rival groups and to enter pubs. Some Casuals also wore clothing similar to those worn by Mods.

Although it did not obtain its name until the 80's, the designer clothing and fashion aspect of the Casual subculture began in the mid-to-late 70s. One well documented precursor was the trend for Liverpool fans starting to dress differently from other fans; in Peter Storm jackets, straight-leg jeans and Adidas trainers. Liverpool supporters were the first British fans to wear continental European fashions, which they picked up while following their teams to matches in Europe.

The other precursor was a subculture known as Perry Boys, which began in the mid 70s as a forerunner to the Casuals. The Perry Boys were Manchester hooligans, who styled their hair into a flick and wore Fred Perry shirts with Dunlop Green Flash trainers.

The Casual style and subculture had no name at first, and was just considered a smart look. It evolved and grew during the early 80s into a huge subculture, reaching its hight around 1982 or 1983, from when the look changed to designer brands such as Armani.

As Islamic immigration began to soar in 2009, several of the more prominent hooligan firms joined together under the Casuals United banner. They are an anti-Islamic protest group that is closely affiliated with the English Defence League (EDL). Both groups hold regular protests against the spread of Islamism, Sharia law and Islamic extremism in Britain.

In the 80s and well into the 90s the government drove a crackdown on football-related violence. While football hooliganism had been a growing concern in some other European countries, British football fans now tend to have a better reputation abroad. Although reports of British hooliganism still surface, the instances now tend to happen at pre-arranged locations rather than at the matches themselves.

Chapter 5.3
The Skinheads.

Before becoming linking with Neo-Nazism, Skinhead culture started among young English and Jamaican working-class communities in London. There were in fact, some black Skinheads, which came as a complete surprise to me during my research for this book.

In the late 1950s the post-war economic boom provided an increased disposable income to young people. Some of them spent that spare income on new fashions and became the Mods. Working class Mods wore practical clothing styles that suited their lifestyle and their employment circumstances: work boots or army boots, straight leg jeans or Sta-Prest trousers, button-down shirts and braces. When they could, the working class Mods bought suits to wear at dance halls, where they listened to Soul, Ska, Bluebeat and Rocksteady music.

Around 1966, a gap developed between the Peacock Mods (also known as Smooth Mods), who were less violent and always wore the latest expensive clothes and the Hard Mods, who wore shorter hair and portrayed a more working class image. Hard Mods became known as Skinheads by about 1968. Their short hair may have been for practical reasons, since long hair could be a liability in factory jobs and streetfights. Skinheads may also have cropped their hair in defiance of the more middle class Hippie culture. Skinhead culture became so popular by 1969 that even the Rock band Slade temporarily adopted the look as a marketing strategy.

As well as retaining many Mod influences, early Skinheads liked Jamaican rude boy styles and culture, especially the music: Ska, Rocksteady, and early Reggae.

The slang terms: Rude boy, Rudie and Rudy originated in 1960s Jamaican street culture and are still used today. In the late 70s, the 2 Tone Ska revival saw the terms Rude Boy and Rude Girl again being used to describe fans of the genre. The Rude Boy subculture began in poorer sections of Kingston, Jamaica and became associated with violent discontented youths. Along with Ska and Rocksteady music, many Rude Boys wore sharp suits, thin ties, and pork pie or Trilby hats, showing an influence from the fashions of American Jazz musicians and Soul music artists.

The violence that sometimes occurred at dances and its association with the Rude Boys gave produced releases by artists who addressed the Rude Boys directly with lyrics that either promoted or rejected Rude Boy violence.

Changing immigration patterns shaped the culture of the time. It was around this time that Jamaican immigrants came to Britain, living side by side with the working class English. This physical proximity offered a chance for cultural exchange and soon English kids latched on to Jamaican Reggae and Ska records. The link between Skinheads and Jamaican music led to the popularity of groups such as Desmond Dekker, Derrick Morgan, Laurel Aitken, Symarip and The Pioneers. The Skinheads started to reject Jamaican music when the tempo slowed down and lyrics became focused on political topics like Black Nationalism and the Rastafarian movement, with which the Skinheads had no affinity. This shift in Reggae's lyrical themes created tension between black and white Skinheads, who otherwise got along fairly well. Around this time, some Suede Heads (an offshoot of the Skinhead subculture) began listening to British Glam Rock bands such as Sweet, Slade and Mott the Hoople.

By 1970, the first generation of Skinheads had started to frighten their peers. The media exacerbated this fear; Richard Allen's 1970 cult novel *Skinhead*; about a racist London skinhead obsessed with clothes, beer, soccer, and violence, is a prime example. Just as we saw the media demonise Teds, Rockers, Mods and Beatniks, they were quick to attack the next emerging youth culture. The second wave of Skinheads didn't take offence at this portrayal; instead, they began to embrace and project it. "*Skinhead*" became the de facto bible for Skinheads outside London, where football fans were quick to take up the subculture.

It didn't take long for political groups to try using the growing subculture for their own ends. The far-right National Front Party saw in the Skinheads a group of working class males whose economic hardships might make them sympathetic to the party's ethno-nationalist politics.

Over time, right-wing efforts to take over Skinhead culture began to rot it from within. For example, Sham 69, one of the most successful Punk bands in the 70s and one who had an unusually large Skinhead following stopped performing altogether after National Front supporting Skinheads rioted at a 1979 concert.

Right-wing nationalists adopted this genre from nearly the very beginning. *Strength Thru Oi!,* is a famous compilation album of Oi! Music, which was named after the Nazi slogan "Strength through joy."

Music and violence became entwined, perhaps best demonstrated in the 1981 Southall riot. On the day two busloads of Skinheads headed to a concert in Southall, which had a large Indian and Pakistani Population. Those Skinheads came across an Asian woman on the way to the concert and kicked her head in, smashing windows and vandalising businesses as they went. Outraged, Indians and Pakistanis followed the skinheads to the pub where the concert was being held. An all-out, racially-charged brawl took place soon after.

By the early 70s, the Skinhead subculture started to fade and some of the original Skins divided into new categories, such as the Suedeheads (defined by the ability to manipulate one's hair with a comb), Smoothies (often with shoulder-length hairstyles), and Bootboys (with mod-length hair; associated with gangs and football hooliganism).

In the late 70s, the Skinhead subculture was after the introduction of Punk Rock. Most of these revivalist Skinheads reacted to the commercialism of Punk by adopting a look similar to the original 1969 Skinhead style. This revival included Suggs, who later formed the band Madness.

From 1979 onwards, Punk-influenced Skinheads with shorter hair and higher boots grew in numbers and grabbed media attention, mostly through football hooliganism. However there still remained some Skinheads who preferred the original Mod-inspired styles.

Most of the first wave Skinheads wore No. 2 or No. 3 grade clip guard cuts (short, but not bald). From the late 70s, they mostly shaved their heads with a No. 2 grade clip or shorter. During that period side partings, or even tennis ball markings, were sometimes shaved into the hair. Since the 80s, some Skinheads clipped their hair with no guard, or even shaved it with a razor.

By the 1970s, most female Skins had mod-style haircuts. During the 80s Skinhead revival, many female Skinheads had feathercuts, short on the crown, with fringes at the front, back and sides.

Skinheads usually wear button-down shirts or polo shirts by brands such as Ben Sherman, Fred Perry, Brutus, Warrior or Jaytex. They might also wear fitted blazers, Harrington jackets, bomber jackets, denim jackets (sometimes splattered with bleach), donkey jackets or Crombie style overcoats.

Traditional Skinheads sometimes wear suits, often in two-tone tonic fabric that changes colour in different light.

Their jeans are worn deliberately short to show off boots. Jeans are sometimes splattered with bleach to resemble camouflage trousers, a style which is popular among Oi! Skinheads.

Many traditionalist Skinheads wear braces, in different colours. Traditionally, braces were worn up in an X shape at the back, but some Oi! Skinheads took to wearing their braces hanging down.

Most Skinheads wear boots; in the 60s they wore army surplus or generic work boots. These were later replaced by Dr. Martens Air Wear boots. In 1960s Britain, the steel-toe boots worn by Skinheads and hooligans were called Bovver Boots; which led to the Skinheads themselves sometimes being called Bovver Boys.

The most popular music style for late 70s skinheads was 2 Tone, a mix of Ska, Rocksteady, Reggae, Pop and Punk Rock. The 2 Tone genre was named after 2 Tone Records, a Coventry record label that represented bands like The Specials, Madness and The Selecter. Some late 70s Skinheads also liked Punk bands, such as Sham 69 and Menace.

In the late 70s, after the first wave of Punk Rock, many Skinheads turned to Oi!, a working class Punk sub-genre. Musically, Oi! combined standard Punk Rock with football chants, Pub Rock and Glam Rock. The term Oi! as a musical genre came from the band Cockney Rejects and journalist Garry Bushell, who championed the band in Sounds magazine.

1980s Skinheads were closely aligned with the first wave of Punk, working class Oi!, Ska, Reggae, 2 Tone Ska, Ska Punk, Dub music, Anarchists and Hardcore Punk.

Members of the second generation in the 80s were often former Punks. Many of them remained fans of Ska and Reggae like the previous generation, but they also listened to and created Punk music. The Skinhead subculture has remained closely connected and overlapping with the Punk subculture ever since.

Chapter 5.4
Northern Soul

If you were an aging Soul musician in the American Deep South during the 1970s, a casino in a depressed town in northern England might be the last place you'd expect to hear your songs played. But that's precisely where a lot of very rare Soul music was playing. The idea of young Brits dancing feverishly to American Soul records might seem a bit far fetched, but affection for black music among the British underclass was well established, as that's exactly where Rock n Roll came from.

Northern England was a rough, grey place, so spinning and gliding around the vibrant, sweaty hotbox of the dance floor was a release to the northern youngsters. The music itself was delivered in the spirited, uptempo swells that are Soul's signature, played loudly by DJs who competed to find the newest, floor-filling tracks.
The Northern Soul scene was typified by a devotion to obscure Soul recordings from small labels like Okeh, Tamla, and Chess. For many fans, the rarer the music, the better they liked it. English record stores began importing American Soul and fans collected and traded vinyl, especially 7" records, or 45s.
The name "Northern Soul" came from the record shop Soul City in Covent Garden, which was run by journalist Dave Godin. It was first publicly used in Godin's weekly column in Blues & Soul magazine during June 1970. In a 2002 interview with *Mojo* magazine, Godin said he first coined the term in 1968, to help staff at Soul City

differentiate the more modern funkier sounds from the earlier and smoother; Motown influenced Soul. Contemporary black music was evolving into what would eventually become known as Funk, but the die-hard Soul fans of Northern England still preferred the mid 60s era of Motown black American dance music. Godin called the Motown style "Northern Soul":

Godin began to notice that northern football fans who were in London to follow their team were coming into the store to buy records, but they did not want the latest tracks in the black American chart. He invented the name as a shorthand sales term. It was just to say 'if you've got customers from the north, don't waste time playing them records currently in the chart, just play them what they like; 'Northern Soul'.

Some Northern Soul records were so rare that only a handful of copies existed, so specific DJs and clubs became associated with particular records that were exclusively in their playlists. As venues evolved into Northern Soul clubs during the late 60s, dancers increasingly demanded newly discovered records. DJs started acquiring rare and often deleted American releases that had not gained even a release in England. These records were sometimes sourced through specialist importers or, in some cases, by the DJs visiting America to buy old warehouse stock.

The venue most often associated with early development of the Northern Soul scene was the Twisted Wheel in Manchester. The club began in the early 50s as a Beatnik coffee bar called The Left

Wing, but in early 1963, the run-down premises were leased by Ivor and Phil Abadi, two Manchester businessmen, and turned into a music venue. At first, the Twisted Wheel hosted mainly live music at the weekend and Disc Only nights during the week. Starting in September 1963, the Abadi brothers hosted all-night parties on Saturday nights, with a mix of live and recorded music.

During the mid 60s, the Twisted Wheel became a focus for Manchester's emerging Mod scene, with a play list that reflected their eclectic tastes in Soul and Jazz. Gradually, the music became less eclectic and shifted heavily towards fast paced Soul, in response to the demands of amphetamine fuelled dancers who attended the all-nighters.

By 1968 the reputation of the Twisted Wheel and the type of music being played there had spread nationwide and Soul fans travelled from all over Britain to attend the Saturday all-nighters.

While Manchester was building a reputation for fast paced Discos, the emphasis in the Midlands was on live Soul bands. Pubs like the Eagle in Birmingham were frequented by young British Soul singers including Steve Winwood and Robert Plant, who both released songs of similar style to early American Soul sounds.

Soul music in America had been exploited by white artists and labels, who profited from covers of songs written by black musicians. In the Northern Soul scene, there was a pride in promoting the work of these undervalued artists. Many of the songs that became hits in Britain had not been popular enough in their home country to support the artists who had written them. In *The*

Story of Northern Soul, Nowell wrote, "Many Northern Soul icons would quit the music business and end up as office janitors, cab drivers, or just plain broke." In their book *Last Night a DJ Saved My Life,* Bill Brewster and Frank Broughton wrote that Northern Soul was a "genre built from failures." Poor, wannabe Motown artists were being picked up by working class kids in places no one cared about. For the Northern Soulies, this simply added to the romance.

As the favoured beat became more up-tempo and frantic, in the early 1970s, Northern Soul dancing became more athletic, looking more like the later styles of Disco and Breakdance. Their routines featured spins, flips, karate kicks and backdrops. Club dancing styles were often inspired by the stage performances of American Soul acts like Little Anthony & the Imperials and Jackie Wilson. The dancers were not paired, as with the many drug-fuelled dance trends that followed, Northern Soul dancing was a solitary trip, shared intimately with the others on the floor. In fact, many of the dance moves pioneered on Northern Soul dance floors influenced Disco and Breakdancing.

A large part of Northern Soul's original audience came from inside the 1960s Mod subculture. In the late 1960s, when some Mods started to follow Freakbeat and Psychedelic Rock, other Mods, especially those in Northern England, stuck to the original Mod sounds of Soul and Blue Beat. From the latter category, two separate sub cultures emerged: Skinheads and Northern Soul. Though early Northern Soul fans were heavily into the Mod look;

Fred Perry and Ben Sherman shirts, with Sta-Prest trousers, or form fitting skirts and dresses, their real passion was for all-night dancing. As a result the clean lines of Mod attire gradually gave way to fuller skirts, baggier trousers and more breathable fabrics. Northern Soul dancers began wearing loose fitting clothes for reasons of practicality. This included high waisted, baggy Oxford trousers and sports vests. These were often covered with sew-on patches representing Soul Club memberships.

The raised clenched fist symbol that became associated with Northern Soul came from the 1960s Black Power movement in America. On his first visit to the Twisted Wheel in 1971, Dave Godin recalled that "... many young fellows wore black "right on now" racing gloves ... between records one would hear the occasional cry of "right on now!" or see a clenched gloved fist rise over the tops of the heads of the dancers".

"Soulies" often carried leather athletic bags bearing stickers and patches from other venues and all-nighters. They were filled with vinyl singles to trade, extra clothes for when their first outfit was soaked in sweat and "blueys," the amphetamines that kept them up and dancing from midnight until morning. After all, a big part of Northern Soul's thrill was flipping the gruelling work day schedule on its head. As one former Soulie said in the 2012 documentary *Keep On Burning: The Story of Northern Soul*, "I was going out when other people were going to bed. For these people, the night is over. For me, it's just beginning."

Many clubs that hosted Northern Soul all nighters didn't open until midnight, which meant they could not get a drink licence. As a result, there was almost a total absence of alcohol in the scene. One Soulie in the documentary *This England: Wigan Casino*, said that he was "slightly embarrassed" to talk to people who weren't in the Northern Soul scene because "they have a total lack of understanding." They couldn't comprehend why anyone would want to drive to a small town like Wigan just to dance to a club with no booze. His friends asked if there are lots of girls at the club. "Yeah, there's a lot of girls there," he reports answering. "They mean plenty of girls there to pick up, but I mean there are plenty of girls there, like, friends."

Northern Soul reached its peak in the mid to late 1970s. By this time, there were Soul Clubs in most major towns of the Midlands and North of England. The three venues regarded as most important were the Golden Torch in Tunstall, Stoke-on-Trent (1971 to 1972), Blackpool Mecca (1971 to 1979) and Wigan Casino (1973 to 1981). Although Wigan Casino is now the most famous, the best attended Northern Soul all night venue at the beginning of the 70s was actually the Golden Torch. Chris Burton, the owner, said that by 1972, the club had a membership of 12,500, and had hosted 62,000 separate customer visits.

Wigan Casino began its weekly Soul all nighters in September 1973. It had a much bigger capacity than many competing venues and ran its events from 2.00am until 8.00am. By 1976, the club had a membership of 100,000 people and in 1978; it was voted the world's number one Discotheque by Billboard Magazine.

Every all nighter at Wigan Casino ended with the playing of three well known songs with a going home theme. These became known as the "3 before 8" and were: "Time Will Pass You By" by Tobi Legend, "Long After Tonight is Over" by Jimmy Radcliffe and "I'm on My Way" by Dean Parrish.

The Twisted Wheel gained a reputation as a drug den and the club closed in January 1971, under pressure from the police and other authorities.

In spite of the drug use, fans thought there was a certain purism to the Northern Soul scene. In his piece, *Northern Soul and Working-Class Culture in 1970s Britain,* Barry Doyle wrote that "traditional northern working class conservatism and respectability" were on display and the demands of dancing all night kept people from looking for trouble. Unlike other British subcultures where violence was commonplace, Northern Soul was characterised by a kind, community spirit. No alcohol meant very few fights and the combination of sweat and Soul produced a euphoria that turned casual fans into obsessive devotees overnight.

In 2007, Andrew Wilson (a lecturer in criminology at the University of Sheffield) published his sociological study, *Northern Soul: Music, drugs and subcultural identity*. This paper details the lifestyle associated with the scene and the widespread use of amphetamines, or speed, by those involved. Wilson argued that, although many did not use drugs, their usage was heavily ingrained in the fast-paced culture, contributing to fans' ability to stay up all night dancing. Many clubs were shut down or refused licences due to concerns by local authorities that Soul nights attracted drug dealers and users.

Among hardcore Northern Soul fans, it was common to see record labels tattooed on their arms and necks: Ric-Tic, OKeh and Vee-Jay. Really extreme Soulies got a drug brand name tattoo: "I'm a Riker liker" was one of the favourites, referring to the pharmaceutical company that made Black Bombers.

A technique employed by Northern Soul DJs, which was copied by their later counterparts, was sequencing records to create euphoric highs and lows for the crowd. Many of the DJs involved in the original Northern Soul movement went on to become important figures in the House and Dance Music scene. Notable among these are Mike Pickering, who introduced House Music to the Haçienda in Manchester during the 80s and dance record producers Pete Waterman, Johnathan Woodliffe, Ian Dewhirst and Ian Levine. The Northern Soul scene went on to influence Disco, and its culture of poular solo DJs inspired the House and electronic music scenes.

When Wigan Casino closed in 1981, many thought that the Northern Soul scene was on the verge of disintegration. However, the 1970s Mod revival, the Scooterboy subculture and the Acid Jazz movement produced a new wave of fans.

Chapter 5.5
Heavy Metal

"We are Motorhead and we play Rock & Roll." This is how the Motörhead front man began all of his stage shows. Lemmy Kilmister must be the only person who thinks his band plays Rock & Roll. The rest of us call it; Heavy Rock, Heavy Metal, or any of the other loosely interchangeable names for their very fast, very loud Rock music. One of Lemmy's favourite descriptions of their music was "everything louder than everything else," which was certainly true when I saw them at Nottingham's Royal Concert Hall. The people sat around us wished they too had brought ear plugs with them.

Heavy Metal developed in the late 60s and early 70s, mostly in Britain, with its roots in Blues Rock. The bands that created Heavy Metal produced a sound, characterised by highly amplified distortion, extended guitar solos and overall loudness. In 1968, three of the new genre's leading acts, Led Zeppelin, Black Sabbath and Deep Purple were founded.

Heavy Metal's guitar style, which was built around distortion-heavy riffs and power chords, traces its roots back to 1950s Memphis Blues guitarists who played a grittier, more ferocious electric guitar sound, on records such as the Kingsmen's version of "*Louie Louie*" (1963) which was later covered by Motorhead.

American Blues music was a big influence on the early British Rockers. Bands like The Rolling Stones and The Yardbirds developed Blues Rock by recording covers of classic Blues songs and speeding up the tempo. As they experimented with their music, they developed what became the hallmarks of Heavy Metal, in particular, its loud, distorted guitar sound.

The Blues Rock drumming style started out as simple shuffle beats on small drum kits. Then drummers began using a more muscular, complex and amplified approach to be heard over the increasingly loud guitars. Singers similarly modified their technique and increased their use of amplification, often becoming very dramatic too.

When mainstream Rock started turning back towards softer sounds in 1968, Acid Rock bands mutated into Heavy Metal acts. One of the most influential bands in this merger of Psychedelic Rock and Acid Rock was British power trio Cream, who developed a massive, heavy sound through unison riffing between guitarist Eric Clapton and bassist Jack Bruce, as well as Ginger Baker's double bass drumming. Their first two LPs, *Fresh Cream* (1966) and *Disraeli Gears* (1967) are regarded as prototypes for what was to become Heavy Metal.

The Jimi Hendrix Experience's debut album, *Are You Experienced* (1967), was also very influential. Hendrix's technique would be emulated by many Metal guitarists and the album's best selling single, "*Purple Haze*", is identified by some as the very first Heavy Metal hit. The Jimi Hendrix Experience was also an influence on a young Lemmy, as he roadied for them, several years before forming

Motorhead.

Critics disagree over who was the first Heavy Metal band. Most credit either Led Zeppelin or Black Sabbath, with American commentators favouring Led Zeppelin and British commentators Black Sabbath.

Birmingham's Black Sabbath had developed a particularly Heavy sound in part due to an industrial accident suffered by guitarist Tony Iommi before co-founding the band. Unable to play normally, Iommi had to tune his guitar down for easier fretting and rely on power chords with their more simple fingering. The bleak working class environment of Birmingham, a city full of noisy factories and metalworking, has itself been credited with influencing Black Sabbath's heavy, chugging, metallic sound and the distinct sound of Heavy Metal in general.

Deep Purple had fluctuated between styles in their early years, but by 1969 vocalist Ian Gillan and guitarist Ritchie Blackmore had led the band toward the Heavy Metal style. In 1970, Black Sabbath and Deep Purple scored major British chart hits with "Paranoid" and "Black Night", respectively. The same year, two other British bands released debut albums in a Heavy Metal style: Uriah Heep with *Very 'Eavy... Very 'Umble* and UFO with *UFO 1*.

During the 80s, Glam Metal became popular through groups like Mötley Crüe and Poison. Thrash Metal broke into the mainstream with bands like Metallica, Megadeth, Slayer, and Anthrax, while other extreme subgenres of Metal such as Death Metal and Black Metal branched off as sub cultural phenomena.

Since the mid 90s different styles further expanded the the genre. These included Groove Metal (with bands like Pantera, Sepultura, and Lamb of God) and Nu Metal (with bands like Korn, Slipknot, and Linkin Park), of which the latter often incorporated elements of Grunge and Hip Hop.

The typical band lineup included a drummer, a bass guitarist, a rhythm guitarist, a lead guitarist and a singer, who may or may not play an instrument. Keyboards were sometimes used to build the fullness of the sound. For example, Deep Purple's Jon Lord played an overdriven Hammond organ. In 1970, John Paul Jones used a Moog synthesizer on Led Zeppelin III. By the 90s, almost every sub genre of Heavy Metal used synthesisers in their line up.

The lead role of the guitar often clashed with the traditional "frontman" role of the singer, creating a musical tension as the two competed for dominance in an affectionate rivalry.

The prominent role of the bass was also key to the Metal sound, and the interplay of bass and lead guitar is a n important element. The bass guitar provided the low-end sound which made the music "Heavy". The bass played a "more important role in Heavy Metal than in any other genre of Rock". Some bands featured the bass as a lead instrument, an approach popularised by Metallica's Cliff Burton in the early 80s. Lemmy of Motörhead was famous for playing overdriven power chords in his bass lines.

The essence of Metal drumming is to create a loud, constant beat for the band. It requires exceptional endurance, as drummers have to maintain considerable speed, coordination and dexterity to play the intricate beats used in Metal.

Visual imagery plays a big role in Heavy Metal. As well as its sound and lyrics, a Heavy Metal band's image is expressed through album cover art, logos, stage sets, clothing, instrument design and music videos.

Long hair is the most distinguishing feature of Metal fashion, which was adopted from the Hippie subculture. According to journalist Nader Rahman, long hair gave Metal fans "the power they needed to rebel against nothing in general."

The classic uniform of the Heavy Metal fan consists of frayed or torn jeans, black T-shirts, boots, and black leather or denim jackets. Fashion and personal style was particularly important for Glam Metal bands. Performers typically wore their hair long and hairspray-teased, used lipstick and eyeliner; wore gaudy clothing, including leopard-skin-printed shirts or vests and tight denim, leather, or spandex pants; and accessories like headbands and jewellery.

Many Metal musicians when performing live engage in head banging, which involves rhythmically beating time with their head, often emphasised by their long hair. Patrons of Metal concerts do not dance in the usual sense. It has been argued that this is due to the music's mostly male audience and "extreme heterosexualist ideology. The performance of air guitar is also popular among Metal fans both at concerts and listening to records at home.

Thrash Metal concerts have two elements that have not become part of the other Metal genres: Moshing and stage diving. Both of which crossed over from the Punk subculture. Moshing involves bumping and jostling each other as you move in a circle around an area called the "pit" near the stage. Stage Divers climb onto the stage and then jump back into the audience.

One of Heavy Metal's biggest influences comes from a very surprising place. A lot of early influence came from Blues and R&B, but Classical Music has also been a big influence since the genre's earliest days. This is probably because many of Metal's most influential artists were guitar players who had also studied classical music. This was certainly true in my own Grammar School, where the School Orchestra's double base player, also played Bass Guitar in a Rock band. Many of Metal's chord progressions and virtuosic practices were taken from 18th century Classical Music, especially Bach and Vivaldi, which were adapted by guitarists including Ritchie Blackmore and Eddie Van Halen.

Even in terms of fan base, the two groups are close in many ways. Adrian North, a Heriot-Watt University professor, found that Metal listeners tended to be creative, at ease with themselves and introverted; which were qualities he also found in Classical listeners.

What is also common between fans of both genres, yet differs from most other groups I have studied, is a lack of violence within their subcultures. You would never expect a gang of Classic listeners to behave like thugs. Perhaps more surprisingly, we rarely see violence orchestrated by the Metal fans either.

There has been a great deal of controversy over the way Black

Sabbath, and the many Metal bands that they inspired, have based their lyrics on dark and depressing subjects. An example is Black Sabbath's second album Paranoid (1970), which included songs dealing with personal trauma; like Paranoid and Fairies Wear Boots, which described the unsavoury side effects of drug- use.

In 1986, Ozzy Osbourne was sued over the lyrics in his song Suicide Solution. A law suit was filed by the parents of John McCollum, a depressed teenager who committed suicide after listening to Ozzy's song. Osbourne was not found to be responsible for the teen's death.

In 1990, Judas Priest was sued in an American Court by the parents of two young men who shot themselves five years earlier, allegedly after hearing the subliminal message "do it" in a Priest song. The case was dismissed.

The origin of the term "Heavy Metal" in a musical context is uncertain. The name might come from "Hippiespeak," where the word "Heavy" was synonymous with "profound" and "Metal" designated a type of mood, weighted as with metal. The word "Heavy" in this context was an element of Beatnik and Hippie slang. References to "Heavy Music," meaning slower, more amplified variations of standard Pop had already become common by the mid 60s.

As you might expect for such a long lasting genre, Heavy Metal has spawned many sub-genres. One of the best examples of artists crossing the sub-genres is Richie Blackmore. He began his career as a session guitarist with revolutionary Producer Joe Meak, playing with a multitude of bands, including Screaming Lord Sutch. But Blackmore matured as a virtuoso soloist with Deep Purple. He left Deep Purple in 1975 to form Rainbow with Ronnie James Dio, the singer and bassist in Blues Rock band Elf and a future vocalist for Black Sabbath. In Rainbow Blackmore expanded on the mystical and fantasy based themes which are often found in Heavy Metal. Blackmore now performs with his partner Candice Knight, in a duo they call Blackmore's Night. Their music is very haunting, with a medieval tone and is very different to what one might expect of a Heavy Metal pioneer.

Punk Rock emerged in the mid 70s as a reaction against the social conditions of the time, as well as the indulgent, overproduced Rock music of the time. Sales of Heavy Metal records declined sharply in the late 70s in the onslaught of Punk, Disco, and more mainstream Rock. Motörhead, founded in 1975, was the first well known band to straddle the Punk / Metal cross over.

The first generation of Metal bands were dropping out of the limelight. Deep Purple had broken up not long after Blackmore's departure in 1975 and Led Zeppelin split following drummer John Bonham's death in 1980.

Many of the surviving bands adopted the theatrics of Glam Metal such as Alice Cooper and Kiss. Glam Metal bands were visually identified by long, overworked hair styles with wardrobes which were sometimes considered cross-gender. The lyrics of these Glam Metal bands tended to emphasise hedonism and wild behaviour.

Their song lyrics usually included sexual expletives and the use of narcotics, very different to early Heavy Metal.

Many subgenres of Heavy Metal developed outside the commercial mainstream in the 80s. Music critic Garry Sharpe-Young's Metal Encyclopaedia separated the underground into five categories: Thrash Metal, Death Metal, Black Metal, Power Metal and the subgenres of Doom and Gothic Metal.

Thrash Metal emerged in the early 80s through the influence of Hardcore Punk and a new wave of British Heavy Metal, particularly songs in a revved-up style called Speed Metal. Thrash has been called "a palefaced cousin of Rap". The subgenre was made popular by the "Big Four of Thrash": Metallica, Anthrax, Megadeth, and Slayer.

There are a multitude of influential and talented bands I could highlight in this chapter. But I am going to indulge myself with telling the story of a man whose career spanned my entire life.

Ian Fraser Kilmister (24 December 1945 – 28 December 2015), better known as Lemmy, was a British singer-songwriter who founded and fronted Motörhead. His nickname came from constant requests for people to "lemmy a quid."

His distinctive gravelly singing voice became one of the most recognisable voices in Rock, along with his style of singing, looking up towards a microphone tilted down towards his weather-beaten face. He was also known for his very distinctive bass playing style, through which he used his Rickenbacker bass to create an "overpowered, distorted rhythmic rumble".

Lemmy was born in Stoke-on-Trent, but grew up in North Wales. He was influenced by Rock & Roll and the early work of the Beatles, which led to him performing with several Rock groups in the 60s. Moving to Stockport, Lemmy joined two local bands, first the Rainmakers and then the Motown Sect who played northern clubs. In 1965, he joined the Rockin' Vickers and signed a deal with CBS, released three singles and touring Europe. Leaving the Rockin' Vickers in 1967, Lemmy moved to London, where he shared a flat with Noel Redding, bassist of the Jimi Hendrix Experience and became a roadie for the band.

In August 1971, Lemmy joined Space Rock band Hawkwind, as a bassist and singer. He had no experience as a bass guitarist and was cajoled into joining immediately before a benefit gig in Notting Hill by bandmate Dik Mik, who's motivation was to add a second band member who enjoyed amphetamines. The other Hawkwind members used marijuana and LSD. He developed a distinctive style that was shaped by his early experience as a rhythm guitarist, often using double stops and chords rather than the single note lines played by most bassists. He also sang lead vocals on several songs, including the band's biggest UK chart single, "*Silver Machine*", which reached number 3 in 1972.

In 1975, Lemmy was arrested at the Canadian border, for drug possession; he spent five days in jail but was released without charge. Never the less, he was fired by Hawkwind. He said the band dismissed him for "doing the wrong drugs".

Now on his own, Lemmy decided to form a new band called Motörhead, inspired by the final song he had written for Hawkwind. Lemmy was the only constant member of Motorhead, the other founding members were: guitarist Larry Wallis and drummer Lucas Fox. The band is often considered a precursor to the new wave of British Heavy Metal, which re-energised the scene in the late 70s and early 80s. Although several guitarists and drummers have played in Motörhead, most of their best-selling albums and singles feature "Fast" Eddie Clarke on guitar and Phil "Philthy Animal" Taylor on drums.

Motörhead released 22 studio albums, 10 live recordings, 12 compilation albums, and five EPs over their 40 year career. Usually performing as a power trio, they had particular success in the early 80s, getting several singles into the UK Top 40. Their albums Overkill, Bomber, Ace of Spades, and No Sleep 'til Hammersmith cemented Motörhead's reputation as a top-tier Rock band. By 2016, they had sold more than 15 million albums worldwide.

Motörhead are usually classified as Heavy Metal and their fusion of Punk into the Rock genre helped pioneer Speed Metal and Thrash Metal. Their lyrics covered such topics as war, good versus evil, abuse of power, promiscuous sex, substance abuse and, most famously, gambling, which was the focus of their hit song "Ace of Spades".

Motörhead has been credited with being part of, or influencing several music scenes, but from the mid-70s onwards, Lemmy insisted they were a Rock & Roll band. Lemmy continued to record and tour regularly with Motörhead until his death in 2015 from prostate cancer. He died in Los Angeles, where he had lived since 1990. Drummer Mikkey Dee and guitarist Phil Campbell both confirmed that Motörhead would not continue as a band.

Chapter 5.6

Hippies

With most of the regularly changing youth cultures, there was rarely anything completely new. One trend would morph into another at varying speeds. It was the same with the Beaten Generation, or Beatniks, whose dark image transformed into something much more colourful. As with many of the cultures, this transition from Beatnik to Hippie happened in America.

Some of the earliest San Francisco Hippies were former students at San Francisco State College who became sucked in by the developing psychedelic Hippie music scene. These students joined the bands they loved, living communally in large, affordable Victorian apartments in the Haight-Ashbury district of San Francisco. Young Americans from around the country started moving to San Francisco and by June 1966, about 15,000 Hippies had moved into the Haight. The Charlatans, Jefferson Airplane, Big Brother & the Holding Company and the Grateful Dead all moved to the Haight-Ashbury neighbourhood during this period.

The bohemian predecessor of the Hippie culture was the "Beat Generation" style of coffee houses and bars, whose customers appreciated literature, a game of chess, Jazz & Folk music, modern dance and traditional crafts and arts like pottery and painting. The entire tone of this new subculture was different. Jon McIntire, manager of the Grateful Dead thought the greatest contribution of the Hippie culture was "this projection of joy. The Beatnik thing was black, cynical, and cold. Hippies sought to free themselves from society's restrictions, choose their own way, and find new meaning in life."

Hippies inherited their cultural dissent from the Beatniks. Beats like Allen Ginsberg crossed over from the Beat movement and became fixtures of the growing Hippie and anti-war movements. The Hippies were one of several dissenting groups of the 60s. They rejected established institutions, criticised middle class values, opposed nuclear weapons and the Vietnam War, embraced Eastern philosophy, championed sexual liberation, were often vegetarian, used psychedelic drugs which they believed expanded the consciousness and created communes. They performed alternative arts, like street theatre, folk music, and Psychedelic Rock as a way of expressing their feelings, their protests and their vision of the world. Their ideology promoted peace, love and freedom, as expressed in The Beatles' song "*All You Need is Love*." Hippies thought the State was a corrupt, monolithic entity that exercised power over their lives, calling this culture "The Establishment," or "The Man."

The word Hippie came from Hipster and was first used to describe the Beatniks who had moved into New York City's Greenwich Village and San Francisco's Haight-Ashbury district. The origin of the term Hip is uncertain, but by the 40s it was part of African American jive slang and meant "sophisticated; currently fashionable; or fully up-to-date." The Beats adopted the term hip and early Hippies inherited their language and countercultural values from the Beat Generation.

By 1965, Hippies were an established social group America and the movement expanded into Britain, Europe, Australia, Canada, New Zealand, Japan, Mexico and Brazil. Hippie culture influenced The Beatles and others in Britain, who in turn influenced their American counterparts. Hippie culture spread worldwide through the fusion of Rock music, Folk, Blues, and Psychedelic Rock.

Following in the footsteps of the Beats, many Hippies smoked cannabis, considering it pleasurable and harmless. They enlarged their spiritual pharmacy with hallucinogens such as LSD and Psilocybin Mushrooms, while often renouncing alcohol.

Their reputation as a protest movement started on October 6th 1966, when California made LSD illegal. In response, San Francisco Hippies staged a gathering in Golden Gate Park, called the Love Pageant Rally, which attracted about 800 people.

Their protesting continued later that year, with the Sunset Strip Curfew Riots, also known as the Hippie Riots. These took place between police and young people on Hollywood's Sunset Strip, between 1966 and the early 70s. In 1966, frustrated residents and business owners encouraged the passing of a strict 10 p.m. curfew and loitering laws to reduce traffic congestion caused by young club patrons. This was seen by the Hippies as an infringement of their civil rights. The *Los Angeles Times* reported that as many as 1,000 young demonstrators, including celebrities Jack Nicholson and Peter Fonda, who was handcuffed by police, attended the protest. The Vietnam War solidified the Hippies reputation for protest in

1971, at the May Day Protests, where 12,000 protesters were arrested in Washington DC. Even President Nixon came out of the White House and chatted with a group of protesters.

On 14th January 1967, the outdoor Human Be-In helped to popularise Hippie culture across America, with 20,000 Hippies gathering in San Francisco's Golden Gate Park. On 26th March 10,000 Hippies gathered in Manhattan for the Central Park Be-In. The Monterey Pop Festival in June introduced Rock music to a wide audience and was the start of the "Summer of Love." Scott McKenzie's rendition of "San Francisco" became a hit and its lyrics, "If you're going to San Francisco, be sure to wear some flowers in your hair", inspired thousands of young people from around the world to head for San Francisco. Many of them wore flowers in their hair and distributed flowers to passers by, earning them the name, "Flower Children".

By the end of the Summer of Love, the Haight-Ashbury scene had begun to deteriorate. The Haight could not accommodate the big influx of naive youngsters with no where to live. Many lived on the street, begging and drug-dealing. Crime and violence sky rocketed, neither of these trends reflecting what the Hippies had envisioned. By the end of 1967, many of the Hippies and musicians who started the Summer of Love had moved on. Beatle George Harrison visited Haight-Ashbury and found it to be a haven for dropouts, which inspired him to give up LSD.
But the decline of Haight-Ashbury did not mark the decline of the

Hippies. In August 1969, the Woodstock Music and Art Fair was held in Bethel, New York, which for many, exemplified the best of Hippie counterculture. More than 500,000 people came to hear some of the most famous musicians and bands of the era, among them Canned Heat, Richie Havens, Joan Baez, Janis Joplin, The Grateful Dead, Creedence Clearwater Revival, Crosby, Stills, Nash & Young, Carlos Santana, Sly & The Family Stone, The Who, Jefferson Airplane, and Jimi Hendrix. It was at Woodstock that many of the Hippies thought their ideals of love and human fellowship gained real-world expression.

Similar Rock Festivals happened in other parts of the country, which helped spread Hippie ideals across America. In December 1969, a Rock festival was held in Altamont, California, 30 miles east of San Francisco. It was initially billed as "Woodstock West", but its official name was The Altamont Free Concert. About 300,000 people came to hear The Rolling Stones; Crosby, Stills, Nash & Young; Jefferson Airplane and other bands. The Hells Angels provided security which proved far less friendly than the security at Woodstock. 18-year-old Meredith Hunter was stabbed and killed during The Rolling Stones' performance after he waved a gun toward Mick Jagger.
In Britain in 1970, a crowd of about 400,000 people gathered at the gigantic Isle of Wight Festival.

By the 70s Hippie culture seemed to be on the wane. The violence at Altamont shocked many Americans, including those identifying with Hippie culture. Another shock came in 1969 when Sharon Tate and Leno & Rosemary La Bianca were murdered by Charles Manson and his "family" of followers. Manson was a long time criminal who was released from prison just in time for San Francisco's Summer of Love. Manson had long hair, huge charisma and the ability to charm a crowd with his guitar playing, singing and rhetoric and he exhibited many of the outward manifestations of Hippie identity. Yet he hardly exemplified the Hippie ideals of peace, love, compassion and human fellowship. Through his twisted logic, hallucinogenic drugs and psychological manipulation, he inspired his followers to commit murder. Manson's highly publicised 1970 trial and subsequent conviction forever tarnished the Hippie image in the eyes of many Americans.

One of the Hippies expression of their independence from society's norms was their style of dress and grooming, which served as a visual symbol of their insistence on individual rights. Through their appearance, Hippies questioned authority and distanced themselves from the "straight" and "square" elements of society. As with some other youth movements, their deviant behaviour included challenging the gender differences of their time: both men and women wore jeans and had long hair. Both genders wore sandals, moccasins or went barefoot. Men often had beards, while women wore little or no makeup and many went braless. Hippies often chose brightly coloured clothing and wore unusual styles, like bell bottom trousers and tie-dyed items. A lot of Hippie clothing was home made in defiance of corporate culture. Hippie homes and vehicles were usually decorated with psychedelic art.

Hippies tended to travel light and could easily pack up and go wherever the action was. Whether at a "love-in" on Mount Tamalpais near San Francisco, a demonstration against the Vietnam War in Berkeley, if the "vibe" wasn't right, Hippies could be mobile at a moment's notice. They were happy to put a few clothes in a rucksack, stick out their thumb and hitchhike anywhere. Hippie households welcomed overnight guests on an impromptu basis and the reciprocal nature of their lifestyle allowed greater freedom of movement.

One travel experience, taken by hundreds of thousands of Hippies between 1969 and 1971, was the Hippie trail, an overland route to India. Carrying little or no luggage and with only small amounts of cash, most followed the same route, hitch-hiking across Europe to Athens and on to Istanbul, then by train through central Turkey, catching a bus into Iran, through southern Afghanistan to Kabul, across the Khyber Pass into Pakistan, then via Rawalpindi and Lahore to the Indian frontier. Once in India, Hippies gathered in huge numbers on the beaches of Goa and Kerala, or crossed into Nepal to spend several months in Kathmandu. In Kathmandu, most of the Hippies hung out in the tranquil surroundings of a place called Freak Street, which still exists today. I visited Freak Street in 2002, on my way into the Himalayas. I was so fed up with a rickshaw riding drug dealer repeatedly offering me an "Afghan reefer Sir?" that my eventual reply "f##k off, I'm a cop," eventually did the trick. India and Nepal drew them because many Hippies rejected mainstream organised religion in favour of a more personal spiritual experience. Buddhism and Hinduism often resonated with Hippies. Some Hippies embraced paganism, especially Wicca. Others were involved with the occult.

Britain also became a popular country for Hippies, particularly while the Beatles were going through their psychedelic phase. The Fab Four were well known for their use of LSD, their song *Lucy in the Sky with Diamonds*, allegedly making cryptic use of the initial letters. The band were also regular visitors to India, following the Hippie's spiritual trail.

Even the Hippies' most recognisable logo, the peace symbol, was developed in Britain. It was designed in England as a logo for the Campaign for Nuclear Disarmament, before being embraced by U.S. anti-war protesters in the 1960s.

Apart from their anti war demonstrations, the American Hippies enjoyed a largely peaceful existence. This was not always the case in Britain, where from the late 60s; Hippies began to come under attack from Skinheads. They were also vilified and sometimes attacked by Punks, Mods, Greasers, Football Casuals, Teddy Boys, Metalheads, Rockers and other youth subcultures of the 70s and 80s.

In Britain, the years between 1987 and 1989 saw a large scale revival of the Hippie movement. This was composed mostly of people aged 18 to 25, who adopted most of the original Hippie philosophy of love, peace and freedom. The summer of 1988 became known as the Second Summer of Love.

Britain's most notable re-run of the Hippie lifestyle was the New Age
Travellers. They were called Hippies by outsiders, but preferred to
call themselves the Peace Convoy. They started the Stonehenge
Free Festival in 1974, but English Heritage banned the festival in
1985, resulting in the Battle of the Beanfield. I cover this particular
offshoot of the Hippies in a later chapter.

Today, Hippies in England can be found in South West England,
around Bristol, Glastonbury, Totnes in Devon, and Stroud in
Gloucestershire, as well as further north at Hebden Bridge in West
Yorkshire and in parts of London and Brighton. In the summer,
many Hippies and similar subcultures gather at various outdoor
festivals in the countryside.

The legacy of the Hippies continues to influence Western society
today. In general, unmarried couples now feel free to travel and live
together without disapproval. Frankness about sexual matters has
become more common. Religious and cultural diversity has gained
greater acceptance. Co-operative business enterprises and creative
community living arrangements are more accepted than before.
Some of the little Hippie health food stores of the 60s and 70s have
become large-scale, profitable businesses, due to greater interest in
natural foods, herbal remedies, vitamins and other nutritional
supplements.

Part 6 - The 1970s

Chapter 6.1
Prog

As the 60s rolled into the 70s a curious hybrid sub genre of Rock emerged. Progressive or Prog Rock was in part a development of the Hippies' Psychedelia, but with a return to Heavy Rock's roots in the Classics.

The fans also seemed to be the natural successors of the earliest Hippies, the university drop outs who gathered together in San Francisco's Haight-Ashbury District. The big difference between the Hippies and the Prog fans was their drug of choice. Any inhibitions the youth of Haight-Ashbury may have had were taken away by LSD. But in 1970s Britain, the Rock crowd were moving away from hallucinogenic drugs, with cannabis becoming their chosen drug. Without LSD, the bright but introverted teenagers left behind the tie dyed clothing of the Hippies, in favour of RAF surplus trench coats or sheepskin Afghan coats. The long hair and flared jeans remained, but everything else was far more sombre than the Hippies' devil may care attitudes.

The final accessory for any self respecting Prog fan was a 12 inch LP record carried under their arm. They might have had nowhere to play it, but the latest double album, with its fantasy art sleeve, was just the thing to advertise your advanced musical taste.

Prog fans at concerts often seemed like upper class Hippie snobs who smoked a lot of pot. They were mostly young men, who would never be described as "chick magnets." They were very bright and very aware that they were very bright, in their late teens and early twenties. At concerts there was always a cloud of smoke hovering in the air and lots of discussion about lyrics and other aspects of their music. The fans still acted like they were at a Rock Concert, but they portrayed a sense that they were in the presence of the most intellectual, virtuosic and sophisticated music on the planet.

Many popular Classic Rock artists, like The Beatles, Queen and Led Zeppelin, dabbled in Prog. Many consider Led Zeppelin's classic track "*Stairway to Heaven*" to be a Progressive Rock song. Likewise, many other lengthy Classic Rock pieces; like The Who's "*Won't Get Fooled Again*" and Dire Strait's "*Tunnel of Love*," fit the genre's profile. Pink Floyd, one of the most famous bands in music history, is a Prog Rock band, though many people are not aware of this.

Genesis, particularly under Peter Gabriel's lead, is probably the earliest of the well known Prog Rock bands. The other big names of the genre all came from Britain; Prog took time catching on in America and was never quite the same as our home grown version.

The most famous of the bands are:

Yes – This band is famous for their complex guitar and keyboard solos. Their songs were often science fiction-themed.

Jethro Tull – A progressive folk group, whose songs featured a lot of folk and acoustic elements. Woodwind was incorporated by their bandleader Ian Anderson and used guitar sounds that ranged from bluesy to heavy.

The Moody Blues – A crossover group who recorded mostly short, straightforward Prog songs featuring classical instrumentation and lyrics that ranged from poetic to amusing to touching.

Emerson, Lake & Palmer – Were a more difficult Prog band to get into, ELP's music was based around the pianos and organs of keyboard player Keith Emerson. Their songs were creatively chaotic and humorously over-the-top.

King Crimson – Like ELP, this band was more difficult to get into, but was considered one of the most important Prog bands of all. Their style was eclectic and sometimes Jazzy with heavy guitars and lots of other instruments thrown into the mix. Like ELP, their music often became very chaotic.

Almost all of the genre's major bands, including Jethro Tull, King Crimson, Yes, Genesis, Van der Graaf Generator, ELP, Gentle Giant and Curved Air, released their debut albums between 1968 and 1970. Most of these were Folk Rock albums that gave little indication of what the band's mature sound would develop into, Prog mostly remained a British phenomenon, as very few American bands played it. Cultural factors played a big part in this, as US musicians tended to come from a Blues background, while Europeans often had a foundation in Classical music.

The best known part of the Prog genre is the Concept Album. These are albums that tell stories and should be listened to from start to finish; to be fully appreciated and enjoyed. Albums like Genesis's *The Lamb Lies Down On Broadway* and The Moody Blues' *Days Of Future Passed* are good examples of classic Concept Albums, all taking the listener on magical adventures with every track playing its part in the experience. My own first Concept Album was *Olias of Sunhillow*. This was a solo project by Yes front man Jon Anderson, released in 1976 (my second year at grammar school). *Olias of Sunhillow* tells the story of an alien race and their journey to a new world to escape a volcanic catastrophe. Olias is the chosen architect of the glider Moorglade Mover, which will be used to fly his people to their new home. Ranyart is the navigator for the glider, and Qoquaq (pronounced 'ko-quake') is the leader who unites the four tribes of Sunhillow to partake in the exodus.

The album represented eight months of recording, but it took two years from its conception to release. Anderson used more than a hundred tracks in putting the album together; overdubbing strings, organ, harp and percussion. The album was inspired by the cover art for the 1971 Yes album *Fragile*, which depicted a tiny planet breaking apart and a glider escaping into space. Another common link to Fragile is the fact that both albums have songs with multiple vocal parts, with Anderson singing all of them. Anderson has said that works by J.R.R. Tolkien and Vera Stanley Alder were also an influence, underlying the epic scope of the album's narrative. Sadly, the album's intricate artwork was lost on me. I have never owned a record player. As a teenager, I used a cassette tape player, then, when CDs entered the market, I swapped to the new media, completely bypassing vinyl. The 5 inch by 3 inch cassette box did a very poor job of displaying the artwork and I had to send off a stamped, addressed envelope to get a printed copy of the narrative. The album peaked at number 8 in Britain and number 47 in America.

Prog is sometimes called Art Rock, Classical Rock or Symphonic Rock. Initially called "progressive Pop", the style was an outgrowth of psychedelic bands who abandoned usual Pop traditions in favour of instrumentation and compositional techniques more frequently associated with Jazz, Folk or Classical music. Other elements also contributed to its "Progressive" label: lyrics were more poetic, new technology was harnessed for different sounds, music approached the status of "art" and the studio, rather than the stage, became the focus for musical activity, which often involved creating music for listening, not dancing. The term "Progressive" referred to a wide range of attempts to break with the standard Pop music formula. The genre coincided with the mid 1960s economic boom that allowed record labels to give greater creative control to their artists. Prog saw a high level of Popularity in the early-to-mid 70s, but began to fade soon after. Conventional wisdom holds that the rise of Punk Rock caused this, but there were other factors contributing to its decline. Music critics also played their part, by labelling the concepts as "pretentious" and the sounds as "pompous" and "overblown." They tended to be hostile towards Prog, or just completely ignored it. After the late 70s, Prog fragmented into numerous forms. Some bands achieved commercial success well into the 80s, with changed line ups and simpler song structures, or alternatively, crossed into Arena Rock.

In 1966, social and artistic connections between British and American Rock musicians dramatically accelerated through bands like the Beatles and the Beach Boys who mixed elements of cultivated music with the traditions of Rock. Early Prog came from the "progressive" Pop groups the 60s like the Beatles and the Yardbirds, who combined Rock & Roll with other music styles like Indian ragas, oriental melodies and Gregorian chants. The Beatles' Paul McCartney said in 1967: "we got a bit bored with 12 bars all the time, so we tried to get into something else. Then came Dylan, the Who and the Beach Boys. ... We're all trying to do vaguely the same kind of thing." This was a time when Rock music began to take itself seriously, paralleling earlier attempts in Jazz, where Swing gave way to Bop.

Bob Dylan introduced a literary element to Rock with his fascination for the Surrealists and French Symbolists, from his immersion in the New York City art scene of the early 60s. The trend for bands with names drawn from literature, like the Doors, Steppenwolf and the Ides of March, was another sign of Rock aligning itself with high culture. Dylan also pioneered blending Rock with Folk music styles. This was followed by Folk Rock groups such as the Byrds, who based their early sound on that of the Beatles. In turn, the Byrds' vocal harmonies inspired those of Yes and British Folk Rock bands like Fairport Convention.

Many groups and musicians played important roles in this development process, but none more so than the Beach Boys and the Beatles. They brought expansions in harmony, instrumentation, duration, rhythm and use of recording technology. Of these elements, the first and last were the most important in clearing a path toward the development of Prog. *Pet Sounds* and *Sgt. Pepper's* used; extended structure, complexity, experimentalism and influences from Classical music. They are viewed as the beginnings of Prog and as turning points from where Rock, which previously had been considered dance music, became music that was made for listening to.

Sgt. Pepper's transformed both musicians' understanding of what was possible and audiences' ideas of what was acceptable in music. Without the Beatles it is fair to say that there would have been no Progressive Rock. In the aftermath of Sgt. Pepper, magazines like Melody Maker drew a line between "Pop" and "Rock', thus separating the "Roll" from "Rock & Roll," a name which now refers purely to the 1950s style.

The September 1974 breakup of King Crimson marked; the beginning of the end, for Prog. Many of the major bands, including Van der Graaf Generator and Gentle Giant disbanded between 1978 and 1980. Many bands had reached the limit of how far they could experiment by the mid 70s and fans had tired of their extended, epic compositions. The sounds of the Hammond, Minimoog and Mellotron had been thoroughly explored and became clichéd. Those bands who continued in the genre often simplified their sound and the genre fragmented from the late 70s onwards.

The era of record labels investing in their artists, giving them freedom to experiment and control over their content and marketing, ended in the late 70s. Corporate staff took back increasing control over the creative process that had, for a time, belonged to the artists. Established acts were pressured to create music with simpler harmony and song structures. A number of symphonic Pop bands, such as Supertramp, 10cc and the Electric Light Orchestra, brought their orchestral style arrangements into Pop singles, while Jethro Tull and Pink Floyd opted for a harder sound in the style of Arena Rock.

Genesis did something even more impressive, transforming themselves into a Top Forty band while also spawning three successful solo careers. The singer, Peter Gabriel, became a Pop star and so did the drummer, Phil Collins, as did the bassist, Mike Rutherford, who led Mike & the Mechanics. For a few of the genre's biggest stars, the music industry offered an attractive bargain: leave Prog behind and you can be bigger than ever.

Chapter 6.2
Punk

Every generation had its own youth sub-culture that shocked the established order of things, but when Punk began in the early 1970s it was the most shocking of them all.

The first bands to take on the recognisable style were the New York Dolls and Television, who both came out of a small New York scene. The New York Dolls were befriended by future Sex Pistols manager Malcolm McLaren. They were outrageously dressed and delighted in disgusting people with Nazi salutes and vomiting in front of cameras. McLaren saw something special in Television as well; especially in their bassist, Richard Hell, whose image of spiky hair and ripped clothes were copied in London by McLaren and have been worn by thousands of Punks since.

On both sides of the Atlantic, young disillusioned white teenagers were looking to escape the boredom and constraints of society, with unemployment, racial tension and social unrest fuelling their fires.

English pub Rock between 1972 and 1975 contributed to the growth of Punk Rock by developing a network of small venues, where less well known bands could play. Pub Rock led to the idea of independent record labels, like Stiff Records, who released basic, low-cost records. Pub Rock bands organised their own small venue tours and made small releases of their records. In the early days of Punk, this DIY method was a marked contrast to what some regarded as the ostentatious musical effects and technological

143

demands of mainstream Rock bands.

Punk remained an underground scene until 1976, when The Ramones and The Sex Pistols made the outside world take notice of them. They became hugely successful in their own right and also inspired others, who realised you, did not have to be able to play an instrument to be in a band; you just needed something to say. Legend has it that after seeing the Sex Pistols, Joe Strummer was inspired to form The Clash. Whatever the truth, the Sex Pistols caused tabloid outrage, using tricks McLaren had learned in New York and the Punk explosion disgusted as many as it inspired.

The term "Punk" was first used by American critics in the early 70s, to describe Garage bands and their fans. The first wave of Punk was aggressively modern, distancing itself from early 70s Rock. According to Ramones drummer Tommy Ramone, "In its initial form, a lot of 60s stuff was innovative and exciting. Unfortunately, what happens is that people who could not hold a candle to the likes of Hendrix started noodling away. Soon you had endless solos that went nowhere. By 1973, I knew that what was needed was some pure, stripped down, no bullshit Rock & Roll."

John Holmstrom, founder of Punk magazine, said "Punk Rock had to come along because the Rock scene had become so tame that Billy Joel and Simon and Garfunkel were being called Rock & Roll, when to me and other fans, Rock & Roll meant this wild and rebellious music."

Neither McLaren, or his partner Vivienne Westwood were performers, but they had a huge influence on boosting the Punk scene. They already owned a London boutique, which first sold Teddy Boy, then Mod clothing. But after their return from New York in May 1975, the boutique was renamed SEX and created the radical Punk clothing style. Vivienne Westwood credits Johnny Rotten as the first British Punk to rip his shirt, and Sex Pistols bassist Sid Vicious as the first to use safety pins. Few of those following Punk could afford to buy the McLaren and Westwood designs worn by the Pistols, so they made their own, widening the 'look' with various styles based on their designs.

Among those who frequented the shop were a band called the Strand, who McLaren managed. The group was after a new lead singer. Another Sex regular, Johnny Rotten, auditioned for and won the job. Adopting a new name, the group performed their first gig as the Sex Pistols on November 6th 1975, at Saint Martin's School of Art. They quickly attracted a small but devoted following, centred on a clique known as the Bromley Contingent (named after the suburb where many of them had grown up), who followed them around the country. With its crude energy and inflammatory, venomous lyrics, the Sex Pistols' debut single Anarchy in the UK established Punk's MO.

There is now a big range of Punk clothing; including deliberately offensive T-shirts, leather jackets and Doc Marten boots. Punk hairstyles include: brightly coloured hair, spiked hair and Mohawks. Cosmetics, tattoos, jewellery and body modification are all routinely worn by Punks. Early Punk fashion adapted everyday objects for artistic effect, items such as leather jackets, were often decorated with paint, pins, buttons and metal studs or spikes. Ripped clothing was held together with safety pins or tape. Ordinary clothing was customised with markers or paint. Black bin liners were worn as dresses, shirts or skirts. Safety pins and razor blades were worn as jewellery. Leather, rubber, and vinyl clothing that the public associated with sexual practices, also became popular. Some Punks wore tight drainpipe jeans, tartan trousers and kilts. Some early Punks displayed a Nazi swastika for shock value, but most contemporary Punks were staunchly anti-racist and more likely to wear a crossed-out swastika symbol than a pro-Nazi symbol.

A classic moment in Punk's history is a 4th July 1976 concert by the Ramones and the Stranglers at the Roundhouse in London. Many of the future stars of the Punk scene were inspired by this show. By the end of 1976, many fans of the Sex Pistols had formed their own bands, including The Clash, Siouxsie and the Banshees, The Adverts, Generation X and X-Ray Spex. Other UK bands emerging at this time included The Damned, The Jam, The Vibrators and The Buzzcocks.

At the end of 1976, the Sex Pistols, The Clash, The Damned and Johnny Thunders & the Heartbreakers united for the Anarchy Tour. Many of these gigs were cancelled by venue owners, after newspapers seized on sensational stories about the antics of both

146

the bands and their fans.

Breaking down the distance between performer and audience is central to a Punk performance and fan participation at concerts is important. First wave Punk bands like the Sex Pistols and the Damned insulted and goaded the audience into intense reactions, such as: can throwing, stage invasion, and spitting or "gobbing". This culture led Punk dancing to deviant forms. Their signature style was the Pogo. Sid Vicious, before he became the Sex Pistols' bassist, is credited with stating the Pogo in Britain at one of their concerts.

Two dances associated with Punk are the Pogo and Moshing. In the Pogo; dancers jump up and down, while either remaining on the spot or moving around; taking its name from the use of a Pogo stick. Pogo was a precursor to Moshing. Moshing or slam dancing is a dance where participants push or slam into each other, usually during a live show. It is generally associated with aggressive genres, like hardcore Punk and Thrash Metal.

Punks adopted glue sniffing because the public perception of sniffing fitted their self-image. Originally used as a cheap high, adult disgust encouraged Punks to use glue sniffing as a way of shocking society. Model airplane glue and contact cement were among the numerous solvents used by Punks for the euphoria and intoxication that inhaling created. Glue was inhaled by putting a quantity of glue in a bag and "huffing", or inhaling the vapour. Liquid solvents were inhaled by soaking a rag with the solvent and sniffing the vapour.

Punk became a national phenomenon in the summer of 1977 and Punk musicians and fans were subject to violent assaults by Teddy Boys and football yobbos. One Ted-aligned band, Don E. Sibley And The Dixie Phoenix, recorded a song called *The Punk Bashing Boogie.*

"I go down town on a Saturday night, Looking for some punks to have a fight, I hate them punks, they're really vile, I kick 'em in bollocks, that's my style,

[Chorus] Punk bashing boogie on a Saturday night, Punk bashing boogie, it sure is right, I kick 'em in bollocks, kick 'em in the head, I kick them punks until they're dead"

In 1979, aged 15, I was talked into jumping on a bus bound for nearby Sutton in Ashfield with a group of Mansfield Teddy Boys. We were supposed to be going "Punk Bashing," but we never found any to bash. The older ring leaders claimed the Punks had hidden from us, but with hindsight, The Bunker Youth Club should not have been difficult to find and I don't think we looked very hard.

The incident that sealed Punk Rock's reputation and notoriety occurred live on Thames Today, an early evening TV show. Sex Pistols guitarist Steve Jones was challenged by the host, Bill Grundy, to "say something outrageous". Jones called Grundy a "dirty fucker" on live television, triggering media outrage. Two days later, the Sex Pistols' Anarchy Tour was cancelled by venue owners in response to the Grundy interview. Some stores refused to stock the records and radio airplay was hard to come by.

Press coverage of Punk misbehaviour grew intense:

On January 4th 1977, The *London Evening News* ran a front-page story about how the Sex Pistols "vomited and spat their way to an Amsterdam flight."

In May 1977, the Sex Pistols achieved even greater controversy (and number two in the singles chart) with *God Save the Queen*. The band had recently hired a new bassist, Sid Vicious, who was seen as exemplifying the Punk image.

In October, the Sex Pistols hit number eight with *Holidays in the Sun*, followed by the release of their first album, *Never Mind the Bollocks, Here's the Sex Pistols*. Inspiring yet another round of controversy, it topped the British charts.

In 1976 "New Wave" was introduced as an alternative name for the Punk scene. The two names were originally interchangeable, but over time, "New Wave" acquired a distinct meaning. Bands like Blondie, Talking Heads, the Cars and the Police were broadening their repertoire, incorporating dance rhythms, and using more polished production. These were specifically called "New Wave" and no longer refered to as "Punk." Some British Punk acts adopted the New Wave label in order to avoid radio censorship and make themselves more palatable to concert organisers.

Bringing elements of Punk music and fashion into less dangerous styles helped New Wave artists become popular on both sides of the Atlantic. New Wave became a catch-all term, encompassing styles such as 2 Tone, Ska, the Mod revival by the Jam, the sophisticated Pop-Rock of Elvis Costello, the New Romantic phenomenon led by Ultravox and Human League.

There are still small groups of die hard Punks around in Britain, but the original Punks, are now middle-aged. The ranting and raving of people like Johnny Rotten, which made them figureheads for a disillusioned generation in the 70s, has now come to make them figures of ridicule.

Chapter 6.3
Disco

Well, you can tell by the way I use my walk
I'm a woman's man: no time to talk
Music loud and women warm, I've been kicked around
Since I was born
And now it's all right, its okay
And you may look the other way
We can try to understand
The New York Times' effect on man
Whether you're a brother or whether you're a mother
You're stayin' alive, stayin' alive
Feel the city breakin' and everybody shakin'
And we're stayin' alive, stayin' alive

Despite always favouring some form of Rock music, those opening lines of the 1977 musical film *Saturday Night Fever* will stay with me forever. Like most teenagers of my generation, I queued at our local single screen cinema, then once inside, tapped my feat to the Bee Gee's *Staying Alive*. The film made a star of John Travolta as Tony Manero, a working-class 19 year old, who spent his weekends dancing and drinking at Brooklyn's 2001 Odyssey Disco. But like most of the boys, I was really there to watch Karen Gorney playing Stephanie Mangano, Travolta's dance partner.

Saturday Night Fever was a massive commercial success; the film helped popularise Disco music around the world and made Travolta a household name. The *Saturday Night Fever* soundtrack by the Bee Gees is one of the best-selling soundtracks of all time. The film showcased the music, dancing and subculture of the Disco era: symphony orchestrated melodies; haute couture styles of clothing; pre-AIDS sexual promiscuity; and graceful choreography.

Somehow, the storyline of Anthony "Tony" Manero resonated with English teenagers. The hero was a 19 year old Italian American from the Bay Ridge area of Brooklyn. Like most of my peers at the time, Tony lived with his parents, and worked at a dead end job. To escape his day to day life, every Saturday night Tony went to his local Disco.

It turned out that there was a very good reason that this American tale was a good fit with English teenage culture. The film was based on a 1976 New York magazine article by British writer Nik Cohn, *Tribal Rites of the New Saturday Night*. In the mid 90s, Cohn admitted to fabricating the article. Cohn was a newcomer to America and a stranger to the Disco scene. Cohn could not make any sense of the subculture he had been assigned to write about. Instead, his character Vincent, who became Tony Manero was based on a very English Mod acquaintance of Cohn's, from London.

Disco originated in the early 70s but stayed urban and underground until the middle of the decade when it started emerging from America's urban nightlife scene, where it had hidden in house parties and makeshift Discotheques. It gradually gained popularity on mainstream radio. Its initial audiences in the America were club goers from the gay, black, Italian, Latino and psychedelic communities in Philadelphia, San Francisco and New York City. Disco was a reaction against the domination of Rock music and the stigmatisation of Dance music by the Rock counter culture. Through Prog, the Rock scene had already moved away from dancing to their tracks, towards music being exclusively for listening to.

In most Disco tracks, strings, horns, electric piano and electric rhythm guitars created a lush background sound. Orchestral instruments like the flute were often used for solo melodies. The lead guitar, which was at the forefront on Rock tracks, was much less common in Disco. Many Disco tracks also used synthesisers, particularly in the late 1970s.

Well known 70s and 80s Disco performers included: Yvonne Elliman, Grace Jones, Diana Ross, Cher, Donna Summer, the Bee Gees, Boney M, Billy Ocean, Chaka Khan, KC and the Sunshine Band, Village People, Gloria Gaynor, Amii Stewart, and Chic.

By the late 70s, most major American cities had thriving Disco club scenes, where DJs mixed a seamless sequence of dance records. Studio 54, a venue popular among celebrities, was a well-known example of a Disco club.

In Philadelphia, R&B musicians and audiences from the black, Italian, and Latino communities adopted some traits from the hippie and Psychedelia subcultures. These included using music venues with a loud, overwhelming sound, free-form dancing, trippy lighting, colourful costumes, and hallucinogenic drugs. As seen in *Saturday*

Night Fever, many Disco goers wore expensive and extravagant.

There was also a thriving drug subculture in the Disco scene, particularly around drugs that enhanced the experience of dancing to the loud music and the flashing lights; like cocaine and Quaalude, or Mandrax, as it was called in Britain.

Quaalude recently returned to the headlines when comedian Bill Cosby admitted giving it to women he wanted to have sex with. In the 1960s it was used to treat insomnia and anxiety, but it did not take long for the potent drug to be misused. In America people could buy them in semi-legal "stress clinics" without needing to visit a doctor. At its height during the 70s, Quaalude was so popular with the Disco crowd, that it earned the nickname "Disco Biscuits". Quaalude also got the reputation of relaxing people so that they could have freer sex, which made them popular on college campuses. Bay City Rollers singer Les McKeown said he was raped at the height of their fame, by another man, after being given Quaaludes. Rolling Stones guitarist Keith Richards also admitted possession of the drug in 1973. Anyone who has seen Leonardo DiCaprio's depiction of a Quaalude binge in The Wolf of Wall Street; during which he can barely speak or walk, may wonder why anyone would take it voluntarily. Regulators eventually stepped in and by 1984, the drug was listed as a Class B drug in Britain, which made its production and distribution illegal.

The term Disco comes from Discothèque, which is French for "library of phonograph records." But it was later used as a term for

154

nightclubs in Paris. During WWII, because of restrictions set in place by the Nazi occupiers, Jazz dance halls in Occupied France played records instead of live music. Eventually many of these Jazz venues had the name Discothèque. By 1959, the term was used in Paris to describe any of these types of nightclub. By 1960 the name was being used in America to describe that type of club and the type of dancing performed in those clubs.

In 1974 there were an estimated 25,000 mobile Discos and 40,000 professional Disc Jockeys in Britain. The DJ was central to 1970's dance culture, but the dancing crowd was no less important and it was the combination of both elements that created the dance floor dynamic. In Disco clubs, a good DJ did not only lead dancers to the dance floor, but he also felt the mood of the dance floor and selected records to suit the energy. Disco era DJs often remixed existing songs using reel-to-reel tape machines and then add in percussion breaks, new sections, and new sounds. DJs selected songs and grooves according to what the dancers wanted, switching from one song to another with a DJ mixer.

Other equipment was added to the basic DJ setup, providing sound manipulations, like reverb, equalisation and echo effects. Using this equipment, a DJ could do effects like cutting out all but the bass line of a song and then slowly mixing in the beginning of another song using the DJ mixer's crossfader.

In the North West of Britain, the Northern Soul explosion which started in the late 60s made the region receptive to Disco. The region's Disc Jockeys were bringing back Disco records from New York City and George McCrae's *Rock Your Baby* became Britain's first number one Disco single.

Also in 1974, Gloria Gaynor released the first side long Disco mix album, which included a re-hash of the Jackson 5's *Never Can Say Goodbye*. Gaynor's own number one Disco hit was *I Will Survive*, released in 1978, which was adopted as a symbol of female strength and as a gay anthem.

In 1975, American singer songwriter Donna Summer recorded a song with producer Giorgio Moroder *entitled Love to Love You Baby*, which contained a series of simulated orgasms. The song was never intended for release but when Moroder played it in the clubs it caused a sensation. Moroder released the record and it went to number two. The 12" single remains a standard in Discos today. The Italian composer Giorgio Moroder is now called the "Father of Disco".

The Bee Gees, brought to fame through *Saturday Night Fever*, showcased Barry Gibb's falsetto voice to produce hits such as *You Should Be Dancing, Stayin' Alive, Night Fever* and *More Than A Woman.*

By the mid 70s, the previous decade's economic prosperity had declined, with unemployment, inflation and crime rates soaring. Like many of the youth cultures before and since, Disco music and dancing provided an escape from depressing economic issues.

The Disco movement was much more than just music. It was also a subculture based around dance clubs and DJs. The New York underground dance scene in which Disco was born, was itself built on the 1960s notion of community, pleasure and generosity, demonstrated by the Hippies.

At the end of the 70s, a strong anti Disco sentiment had developed among Rock fans and Rock musicians, particularly in America. They called Disco; "mindless, consumerist, overproduced and escapist". The slogans "Disco sucks" and "death to Disco" became common. The Punk subculture too was hostile to Disco. Although many early Sex Pistols fans like the Bromley Contingent quite liked Disco, congregating at Louise's nightclub in Soho and the Sombrero in Kensington. Their film *The Great Rock & Roll Swindle* and its soundtrack album contained a Disco medley of Sex Pistols songs, entitled Black Arabs and credited to a group of the same name.

July 12th 1979, became known as "the day Disco died" because of Disco Demolition Night, an anti Disco demonstration at a baseball game in Chicago. Rock station DJs Steve Dahl and Garry Meier, along with Michael Veeck, the son of Chicago White Sox owner Bill Veeck, staged the promotional event for disgruntled Rock fans. The event involved exploding Disco records and ended with a riot, during which the crowd tore out seats and lumps of turf. The Chicago Police made several arrests and the extensive damage to the field forced the White Sox to forfeit their next game to the Detroit Tigers. The anti Disco backlash, combined with other society and music industry factors, changed the look of Pop radio in the years following

Disco Demolition Night. Starting in the 80s, Country Music began a slow rise through the American Pop charts. Emblematic of Country's rise into the mainstream was the 1980 movie *Urban Cowboy*. Somewhat ironically, the star of the film was John Travolta, who only three years before had starred in *Saturday Night Fever*.

Many factors have been cited as aiding the decline of Disco, including economic and political changes at the end of the 70s, along with burnout from the hedonistic lifestyles led by the fans. In the years after Disco Demolition Night, some social commentators described the backlash as macho, bigoted and an attack on non-white and non-heterosexual cultures. Gloria Gaynor argued that the music industry supported the end of Disco because Rock music producers were losing money and Rock musicians were losing the spotlight. However, despite the backlash, Disco remained relatively successful into the 80s, with big hits like Irene Cara's *Flashdance... What a Feeling*, Michael Jackson's *Thriller*, K.C. and the Sunshine Band's hit, *Give It Up* and Madonna's first album, which contained strong Disco influences.

Giorgio Moroder's soundtracks to movies: *American Gigolo, Flashdance and Scarface* proved that Disco was still very much alive.

Disco's greatest legacy was its influence in the later development of electronic dance music and house music.

Chapter 6.4

Rude Boys

One of the odd paradoxes of 1970s youth culture was the Rude Boys, where violent beginnings in Jamaica found a softer revival in England.

The 2 Tone Ska scene in England saw Rude Boy and Rude Girl being used to describe Ska fans. Bands like the Selector and Madness gave a harmless, almost comical image to the young men in sharp suits, thin ties, and pork pie hats. But there was a darker origin to the originally Jamaican subculture, where Rude Boy and Rudie, or Rudy were slang terms originating in 1960s Jamaican street culture.

The Rude Boy subculture rose from the poor sections of Kingston, Jamaica and its violent discontented youths. Along with Ska and Rocksteady music, many Rude Boys were influenced by the fashions of American Jazz musicians and Soul music artists. By the 70s, Reggae had replaced Ska and Rocksteady as the Rude Boys' music of choice.

It was the violence at dances and its association with the Rude Boy lifestyle that produced a number of releases that addressed the Rude Boys directly with lyrics that either promoted or rejected their violence. Towards the end of 1963 Bob Marley and the Wailers released their first single, *Simmer Down*. The song was written and performed by 18 year old Bob Marley. The lyrics were meant to placate his mother who was worried about the company he kept in the Trench Town ghetto of the Jamaican capital. *Simmer Down* was aimed directly at the sharply dressed young men known locally as Rude Boys, who were making headlines with their violent and antisocial behaviour. "*Simmer down, oh control your temper. Simmer down, for the battle will be hotter,*" sang Marley.Marley's plea for calm was in stark contrast to the Rappers of today, who appear to glorify the culture of violence.

Taking their cue from "baddies" in Hollywood western and gangster movies, the Rude Boys struck fear into respectable Jamaicans, but they attained a level of respect in the ghettoes where they fiercely defended their turf from rival gangs. They also made their presence known at early Ska and Bluebeat sound-system dances, either as hired protection or as rampaging troublemakers.

This was the competitive and violent culture that the Wailers stepped into when they recorded *Simmer Down* in 1963, but the song soon took on a life of its own.

American music journalist Timothy White wrote in *Catch a Fire*, his 1986 biography of Bob Marley, the main reaction to the song in the ghettoes of Kingston was "a communal shock of self-recognition". Despite its cautionary tone, *Simmer Down* became a big seller and paradoxically, much beloved by the very people it criticised. The Rude Boys were increasingly staking their claim in the cut-and-thrust world of Jamaican music. "The militant Rudies got bolder as *Simmer Down* got bigger," wrote White.

Throughout the 60s, Rude Boys were a constant presence in Jamaican music, whether employed as protection by the producers or to disrupt rival sound-system dances.

In the 1960s Jamaican immigration introduced Rude Boy music and fashion to Britain which in turn influenced the existing Mod and Skinhead subcultures. In the late 70s, the name Rude Boy and its associated fashions came back into use after the Specials and their record label 2 Tone Records started a brief but influential Ska revival.

While the Rude Boys were being reinvented as a symbol of multicultural Britain, many of the original Jamaican Rude Boys had become enforcers for the two main political parties in Jamaica: the Jamaican Labour party and the People's National party. By the late 70s, the turf wars of old had escalated into sectarian feuds that left hundreds dead. In many ways, the journey of the Rude Boy from young delinquent to fully fledged gangster heralded the rise of Hip Hop bad guys, like: Ice T and Tupac Shakur, who created the violence of Gangsta rap two decades later.

Of all the artists I could showcase in this chapter, one man stands head and shoulders above the rest for his contribution to world music. Robert Nesta "Bob" Marley (6 February 1945 – 11 May 1981) became an international icon by blending Reggae, Ska and Rocksteady in his music.
Usually thought of as a strictly black icon, Marley was actually mixed race. His father, Norval Marley was a white Jamaican from Sussex, whose family had Jewish origins. Norval claimed to have been a

Captain in the Royal Marines, although at the time of his marriage to Cedella Booker, an Afro-Jamaican, he worked as a plantation overseer.

When Bob Marley was just 10 years old, his father died from a heart attack. Then, two years later, Marley and his mother left Nine Mile and moved to the Trenchtown district of Kingston. The move to Trenchtown proved to be fortuitous, as Marley soon joined a vocal group with Bunny Wailer and Joe Higgs. Marley and the others did not play any instruments at this time and wanted to be a vocal harmony group. Higgs helped them develop their vocal harmonies and started to teach Marley how to play guitar.

In 1963, Bob Marley, Bunny Wailer, Peter Tosh, Junior Braithwaite, Beverley Kelso and Cherry Smith were called the Teenagers. They later changed the name to the Wailing Rudeboys, then to the Wailing Wailers. Their single *Simmer Down* became a Jamaican number one in February 1964 selling an estimated 70,000 copies.

In 1972, Bob Marley signed a contract with CBS Records in London and began a UK tour with American Soul singer Johnny Nash. While in London, Island Records offered of an advance of £4,000 to record an album.

The Wailers' first album for Island, *Catch a Fire*, was released worldwide in April 1973. It was packaged like a Rock album with a unique Zippo lighter lift-top. Initially selling 14,000 units, it did not make Marley an instant star, but it received a positive critical reception. It was followed later that year by the album *Burnin'* which included the track *I Shot the Sheriff*. Eric Clapton was given the album by his guitarist George Terry. Clapton was impressed and recorded a cover version of *I Shot the Sheriff*, which became his first American hit since *Layla* two years earlier, reaching number one on the Billboard Hot 100.

In 1975, Marley had his international breakthrough with his first hit outside Jamaica, *No Woman, No Cry*.

At the end of 1976, after being shot in a politically motivated attack, Marley left Jamaica. Then, after a month long recovery and writing break in the Bahamas, he arrived in England spending two years in self-imposed exile. While in England, he recorded the albums *Exodus* and *Kaya*. *Exodus* stayed in the British album charts for 56 weeks. The album included four UK hit singles: *Exodus, Waiting in Vain, Jamming and One Love*, a rendition of Curtis Mayfield's hit, *People Get Ready*.

In July 1977 Marley was diagnosed with a type of malignant melanoma under one of his toe nails.

Marley's album *Uprising* was released in May 1980. The band completed a tour of Europe, where its biggest concert to 100,000 people, was held in Milan. After the tour Marley went to America, where he performed two shows at Madison Square Garden in New York as part of his Uprising Tour. Marley's last concert was at the Stanley Theatre in Pittsburgh on 23rd September 1980. Shortly afterwards, his health deteriorated as the cancer had spread throughout his body. He died on 11th May 1981 at Cedars of

Lebanon Hospital in Miami, aged 36. His final words to his son Ziggy were "Money can't buy life."

On 21 May 1981, Jamaican Prime Minister Edward Seaga delivered a funeral eulogy for Marley, declaring: "His voice was an omnipresent cry in our electronic world. His sharp features, majestic looks, and prancing style a vivid etching on the landscape of our minds. Bob Marley was never seen. He was an experience which left an indelible imprint with each encounter. Such a man cannot be erased from the mind. He is part of the collective consciousness of the nation."

Chapter 6.5
Hip Hop

By now you will have gathered that although my roots are in Rock music, I also have a more eclectic taste. I enjoy listening to the better examples of many different genres. But, there has been one genre for which I have developed quite a strong distaste. Some of the earliest examples of Hip Hop, I still enjoy, but what it has developed into since its beginning in the 70s is really not my thing. Despite my opinion, National Geographic called Hip Hop "the world's favourite youth culture" and said "just about every country on the planet seems to have developed its own local rap scene."

Hip Hop as a subculture and art movement was born in New York's South Bronx, during the late 1970s. It emerged from neighbourhood block parties thrown by the Ghetto Brothers, a Puerto Rican group who have been variously described as a gang, a club and a music group. They hot wired their amplifiers into the lampposts on 163rd Street and Prospect Avenue and used their live music events to break down racial barriers between African Americans, Puerto Ricans, Whites and other ethnic groups in the Bronx. Jamaican immigrant DJ Kool Herc also played a big role in developing Hip Hop music. On Sedgwick Avenue, Herc mixed samples of existing records and inserted percussion breaks, mixing this music with Jamaican style "toasting" (a style of chanting and boastful talking over a microphone) to rev up his crowd and the dancers. Kool Herc is sometimes called the "Father" of Hip Hop for developing the signature DJ techniques that, along with Rapping, formed the foundation of the Hip Hop music style.

Keith "Cowboy" Wiggins, from Grandmaster Flash and the Furious Five, was credited with inventing the term Hip Hop in 1978. He teased a friend who had joined the US Army by scat singing the made up words "hip / hop / hip / hop" in a way that mimicked the cadence of marching soldiers. Cowboy later worked this "Hip Hop" cadence into his stage performance.

The role of the MC was originally as Master of Ceremonies for a DJ dance event. The MC would introduce the DJ and then try to rev up the audience. The MC made his announcements between the DJ's songs, urging the crowd to get up and dance. MCs also told jokes and used their energetic language and enthusiasm to pump up the crowd. Eventually, their introducing role developed into longer sessions of spoken, rhythmic wordplay, which eventually became rapping.

There is also a tentative link to Rap having African roots. Centuries before Hip Hop existed; the Griots of West Africa told their stories rhythmically, over drums and sparse instrumentation. There are clear similarities between the two cultures, but no hard evidence of the Bronx performers being aware of their African predecessors.

Street gangs were prevalent in the poverty stricken South Bronx and much of the graffiti, rapping, and break dancing in the Bronx were artistic variations on the one-upmanship between street gangs. By this time, Britain had largely consigned its organised gangs to history, in the days of the Scuttlers and Peaky Blinders. But the importation of Hip Hop from New York brought back the gangs back to British streets.

Criminality in New York gave Hip Hop another boost after the 1977 blackout. This blackout saw widespread looting, arson and citywide disorder especially in the Bronx, where looters stole DJ equipment from electronics stores. Using stolen equipment, the Hip Hop genre, which was barely known outside of the Bronx at the time, grew at an astounding rate from 1977 onward.

In late 1979, Blondie's Debbie Harry took Nile Rodgers of Chic to a New York Hip Hop event, where the main backing track used was the break from Chic's *Good Times*. The new style influenced Harry, and led to Blondie's 1981 hit single *Rapture*, which became the first single containing Hip Hop elements by a white artist to reach number one in America. The song itself is considered new wave and mixes Pop music elements, but there is an extended Rap by Harry towards the end. The lyrics used then were still benign phrases, like "the man from Mars is eating cars", unlike the violent lyrics that were to come.

With the commercial success of Gangsta Rap in the early 1990s, the lyrical content shifted to drugs, violence, and misogyny. Hip Hop lyrics are considered controversial for containing swear words. In particular, the word "bitch" is seen in countless songs, from NWA's (Niggaz Wit Attitudes) "*A bitch iz a bitch*" to Missy Elliot's "*She is a bitch.*" Hip Hop has been censored on TV and radio because the graphic descriptions of violence and sex made it hard to broadcast. As a result, many Hip Hop recordings were broadcast in censored form, with the offending language "bleeped" or replaced with "clean" lyrics.

Gangsta Rap is a subgenre of Hip Hop that reflects the violent culture of inner-city black America. The genre began the mid 80s with Rappers such as Ice-T and N.W.A. After the International attention they created in the late 80s and early 90s, Gangsta Rap became the most lucrative sub genre of Hip Hop.

N.W.A's lyrics were more violent, confrontational, and shocking than those of earlier Rap acts. They featured incessant profanity and use of the word "nigga". Their first album was *Straight Outta Compton*, released in 1988. It sparked major controversy when their song "*Fuck tha Police*" attracted a letter from FBI Assistant Director Milt Ahlerich, strongly expressing law enforcement's resentment of the song.

Controversy also surrounded Ice-T's song *Cop Killer*. The song was meant to speak from the viewpoint of a criminal getting revenge on cops. The song outraged: government officials, the National Rifle Association and police advocacy groups. Consequently, Time Warner Music refused to release Ice-T's next album *Home Invasion*.

N.W.A (an abbreviation for Niggaz Wit Attitudes) were among the earliest popular performers of Gangsta Rap. Active from 1986 to 1991, they created controversy over explicit lyrics, which were disrespectful to women and glorified drugs and crime. They professed a deep hatred of the police, which sparked controversy over the years. The group was banned from many American radio stations. Despite this, they sold over 10 million units in America alone. *Straight Outta Compton* was also one of the first albums to adhere to the new Parental Advisory label scheme, which was then still in its early stages: the label at the time consisted of "WARNING: Moderate impact coarse language and / or themes." But, the taboo nature of N.W.A's lyrics just boosted its appeal. Media coverage compensated for N.W.A's lack of airplay and the album went double platinum.

Hip Hop and Gangsta Rap have been regularly criticised for their negative attitude to women. Artists such as Eazy-E, Dr. Dre and Snoop Dogg all have lyrics that portray women as sex toys and as inferior to and dependent on men. Between 1987 and 1993, more than 400 Hip Hop songs had lyrics about violence toward women including rape, assault, and murder. The portrayal of women in Hip Hop music videos also tends to be violent, degrading and highly sexualised. Videos portray idealised female bodies and depict women as being objects of male pleasure. For example, the video for *Tip Drill* by Nelly showed images of a man swiping a credit card between a stripper's buttocks. Hip Hop has also been criticised for homophobia, with lyrics containing offensive terms like "faggot."

Like practically all of the youth cultures that went before, clothing, hair and style became a big part of Hip Hop. Although the styles changed over the decades, distinctive urban clothing and styles have been the look through which Rappers and the Hip Hop community expressed themselves. As the genre's popularity grew, so did the effect of its fashion. There were some early items synonymous with Hip Hop that crossed over into mainstream culture, like Run-DMC's liking for Adidas or the Wu-Tang Clan's championing of Clarks' Wallabees, but it wasn't until its commercial peak that Hip Hop fashion became influential. Begining in the mid- to late 90s, Hip Hop embraced major designers, like: Ralph Lauren, Calvin Klein and Tommy Hilfiger.

This chapter covers the birth of Hip Hop in New York during the 1970s and its spread around the world during the following decades. But Rap did not reach Britain until the 1980s and did not gain widespread popularity until the Gangsta Rap of the 1990s. So, I will leave the discussion here and pick it up again in a later decade.

Part 7 - The 1980s

Chapter 7.1
New Age Travellers.

In this chapter, we pick up the story of the Hippies again, in their very British incarnation of New Age Travellers, or "Crusties," the name their unkempt appearance earned them.

The New Age Travellers, or Peace Convoy, as they preferred to call themselves, espoused Hippie beliefs and travelled around, between music festivals and fairs. In order to live in a community with others who held similar beliefs, they lived and travelled in vans, lorries and busses, which they had converted into mobile homes.

The movement began in the free festivals of the 1970s; like the Windsor Free Festival, Glastonbury, Elephant Fayres and the huge Stonehenge Free Festivals. However, they were just the latest in a long line of travelling cultures in Britain. Their predecessors had, included travelling pilgrims and, itinerant journeymen.

During the 80s the Travellers and their mobile homes moved in convoys. They attracted significant opposition from the Government and the media, demonstrated by the authorities' attempts to prevent free festivals at Stonehenge and the resulting Battle of the Beanfield in 1985; the largest mass civil arrest in English history. In 1986 and the years that followed, police continued to block Travellers from "taking the Stones" on the Summer Solstice. This led Travellers to spend summers squatting in their hundreds on sites adjacent to the A303 in Wiltshire.

The Stonehenge Free Festival ran from 1974 to 1984 at Wiltshire's famous prehistoric monument of Stonehenge. The festival traditionally ended with the summer solstice in June each year. By the 1980s, the festival had grown into a major event. The festival crowd were viewed as Hippies by the British public, which along with widespread drug use, resulted in restrictions on access to Stonehenge. Fences were built around the stones in 1977 and police used a historic law against driving over grassland to levy fines against festival goers in motorised vehicles. The festival was a celebration of various alternative cultures: The Tibetan Ukrainian Mountain Troupe, The Tepee People, Circus Normal, the Peace Convoy, New Age Travellers and the Wallys were all regular attendees from the counter culture.

The stage played host to many bands from a wide variety of genres, including: Hawkwind, Doctor and the Medics, Buster Blood Vessel, The Selecter, Dexys Midnight Runners, The Thompson Twins and Wishbone Ash, who all played the festival for free.

In 1984 the Department of the Environment handed management of Stonehenge and its surrounding land to English Heritage. By that time the festival had grown in size and the attendance figure for the 1984 festival was estimated at 100,000. Due to the high attendance figures and the low numbers of police present, they were unable to shut the Festival down or enforce the law. Consequently, illegal drugs were widely available and openly advertised for sale. Traders at the festival neglected to obtain licences or pay taxes. Critics claimed that the 1984 festival resulted in destruction of archaeological remains and to parts of the site itself; the media claimed that "holes had been dug in Bronze Age barrows for toilets and as ovens. Fences had been torn down, and a thousand young trees cut down for firewood". The clean-up cost more than £20,000, in addition to the incalculable cost of lost archaeological information. A High Court injunction was imposed banning the 1985 festival from taking place.

The Battle of the Beanfield happened on 1 June 1985, when Wiltshire Police blocked The Peace Convoy of several hundred New Age Travellers, from setting up the Stonehenge Free Festival. The police were enforcing a High Court injunction obtained by the authorities prohibiting the Festival from taking place. 1,300 police officers took part in the operation against about 600 Travellers.

After spending the night in Savernake Forest, the Convoy on the morning of 1st June numbered about 140 vehicles. It was estimated to contain 600 people. The police had set up an exclusion zone four miles around Stonehenge, which the Convoy hoped to breach. The Convoy met resistance at a police roadblock near Shipton Bellinger about seven miles from Stonehenge. This was created by tipping three lorry loads of gravel across the road. According to The Observer, the convoy avoided the roadblock on the A303 by slipping down a side road but were then met with a second roadblock. At this point the police claim that Traveller's vehicles rammed police vehicles in an attempt to cross the roadblock. Most Travellers drove into an adjacent field, by smashing through a hedgerow, leading to another stand off. Travellers made attempts to negotiate with police but the officer in charge, Assistant Chief Constable Lionel Grundy, ordered that all Travellers be arrested. There were outbreaks of violence during which dozens were injured, with eight police officers and 16 Travellers being hospitalised. 537 Travellers were eventually arrested, representing one of the biggest mass arrests of civilians in English legal history. There were insufficient cells in local police stations to hold all those arrested. Prisoners were transported throughout the Midlands and northern England.

The UK miners' strike had ended earlier the same year and police compared this event with tactics used at the Battle of the Beanfield, stating: "The Police operation had been planned for several months and lessons in rapid deployment learned from the miners' strike were implemented."

The Earl of Cardigan added his take on the disorder, as when the Travellers left Savernake Forest, which is owned by the Earl's family, he decided to follow on his motorbike. The Earl said that during the initial confrontation there were negotiations with police who insisted that the Travellers would not be allowed to pass. The Travellers then began entering a field and "Police rushed out on foot, from behind their barricades. Clutching drawn truncheons and riot shields, they ran round to the driver's door of each vehicle, slamming their truncheons into the bodywork to make a deafening noise, and shouting at every driver, 'get out, get out, hand over your keys, get out." He said that police "smashing up vehicles" and giving instructions to "Get out!" often happened simultaneously, giving the Travellers little time to react before using riot sticks to break the vehicles' windscreens.

Several musicians went on to memorialise the incident in song: The Hawkwind song *Confrontation* includes a description of the day's events and includes a dramatised some of the events including the repeated phrase "I am not interested in anything you have to say." The Levellers' song *Battle of the Beanfield* was inspired by the disorder. *Itinerant Child*, by Ian Dury & The Blockheads, was inspired by Dury's own experiences during the incident.

Many people saw the Castlemorton Common Festival in 1992 as a significant turning point for New Age Travellers in Britain. This was a weeklong festival attracting about 30,000 Travellers and Ravers. The Festival directly resulted in the government enacting new powers for police and local authorities under the Criminal Justice and Public Order Act 1994, to prevent such events in the future. The Criminal Justice Act included powers to combat disruptive trespass, squatting and unauthorised camping. The new powers made life increasingly difficult for Travellers and many left Britain for Ireland and mainland Europe, particularly Spain.

However, thousands of people still live a Traveller lifestyle in Britain. Now known simply as Travellers, they stay on unauthorised sites throughout the UK, particularly in Wales and the south-west of

England. London also hosts a number of Traveller sites in disused factory and warehouse yards and there is often some crossover between Travellers and squatters, with Travellers parking up in yards attached to squatted buildings. A typical Traveller site might have between five to 30 vehicles on it, including trailers and caravans as well as buses, vans and horse boxes converted to live in. Although most Travellers in Britain are British, large numbers of Continental Europeans also "travel" in the UK.

Although New Age Travellers only took to the road in the 1960s, many Traveller families have now reached their third or fourth generation. Not all Travellers live on state handouts; there are some who do seasonal or temporary work on farms and building sites. Others work as self employed mechanics, or make money selling scrap, or running stalls at markets and car boot sales. Summer Festivals also present opportunities for Travellers to make money through offering entertainment, services and goods to Festival goers. The Travelling communities exhibit high levels of mutual aid, such as: the sharing of childcare and vehicle maintenance and "skipping" (collecting food from supermarket skips), which allows them to live on very low incomes. The Traveller and Free Party scenes often have close links, and many Travellers are involved with the sound systems at Raves and squat parties. Raves or huge illegal parties became a problem in the 1990s, as the drug fuelled Disco crowd joined forces with the Travellers, in a new incarnation of the Free Festival.

Chapter 7.2
The New Romantics

The 1980s are remembered for some very strange, over the top fashion. Clothing for both men and women became very flamboyant and hair became very big.

The most amusing 80s story I heard, was from a nurse friend of mine. A trauma team from a London hospital had visited our local hospital to experience the injuries suffered by miners in the Nottinghamshire coalfield. The New Romantic craze had just got going in London, but was yet to gain any real ground in the north. The medics passed comment on the New Romantic eye makeup, worn by so many of the men in casualty. When the local nurses stopped laughing, they explained it was coal dust ingrained into the miners faces. Most of them would have been mightily offended at the suggestion that they wore makeup.

Many of the British youth cults I have featured in this book started in America and gradually worked their way into our culture. This was not so with the New Romantics, which was a very British invention and could be traced back to a single man. That man was Steve Strange. He would eventually go onto front the band Visage, but he began by promoting a dance night at London's Blitz nightclub on a single night each week. Strange came to the media's attention when he expanded his one night per week Blitz calendar with a cabaret night on Thursdays. In his pre event promotion, he described his debut act as "a really great new band, who combine synthesised dance music for the future with vocals akin to Sinatra, they're called Spandau Ballet and they're going to be really big." Spandau Ballet would define a change in direction for music, shifting its driving rhythm from the guitar to the bass and drum. They also made it hip to play Pop music. Within three years Spandau Ballet became leaders of a cult along with three other British groups; Duran Duran, Culture Club and Wham. They led the way for dozens of stylish young club land acts into the charts. Critics said that a backward record industry was completely unaware of the vast dance underground, which was desperate for a revolution in club culture. Every Tuesday for a year, Strange had been holding a "private party" in the shabby Blitz wine bar off Covent Garden. Outrageous dress sense secured entry to the party. Inside, precocious youngsters posed away in outlandish clothes, over the top make-up and haircuts that made you feel that normality was odd. The soundtrack to this self-styled "electro-diskow" was European Disco; synth-led, but bass-heavy. Bands like Kraftwerk, Gina X, Giorgio Moroder and Bowie were played. Robot sounds inspired dancers to pose their angle poise limbs and unmoving chins.

Spandau bassist Martin Kemp only learned to play because his big brother asked him to. But he was part of the Blitz crew. He used to say: "I'm not really a musician. But I belong in a club dressed as sharp as a razor. That's the thrill; just being there at 3 am, excited by where you are and the people sharing the night with you. When Steve Strange eyeballed you at the door of his club, your look alone did not guarantee admission. He did not want passive consumers but "people who created unique identities".

It took a year before the media caught onto what was happening. The national press came up with a few names: New Dandies, Romantic Rebels and the Blitz Kids. Finally, in September 1980 they found the name that stuck, when the music weekly Sounds headline read "New Romantics".

Blitz suddenly became a publicity machine for the posers' age. Attendance at Blitz became a statement of intent; to lead a life of style all week. When Bowie visited the Blitz he recruited four of the kids to dance with his pierrot on the video for *Ashes to Ashes*. It earned each of them £50 and helped Bowie to No 1.

It was inevitable that an unknown band would emerge from Blitz's ranks. Spandau Ballet sounded very un-Rocklike by playing the new synthesised electro-Pop and singing about being very young. Their song writer, Gary Kemp claimed: "We are making the most contemporary statement in fashion and music."

Spandau Ballet were another band that began during a period of social depression in England. Margaret Thatcher came to power in the election of May 1979, but the term "Thatcherism", describing her goal to create "Popular Capitalism", did not come into general use until her second term. Spandau Ballet emerged during the remaining spasms of the previous Labour government's "Winter of Discontent". Times were hard and the future looked desperate as unemployment rose towards three million. Even graduates faced the prospect of no job to go to. This trend was at its worst in the south east, where unemployment among school leavers doubled during 1979 alone. "The city was broken," said Gary Kemp, talking about London, "it was a horrible place." The record industry had stalled, sales were falling and the charts were bland.

Their schoolmate turned manager, Steve Dagger, spent his childhood in the Swinging 60s with the buzz that the Mods brought to Soho. Dagger said "I badly wanted a new swinging London. There had to be a way..."

The press described Dagger as the Svengali behind the rise of the Angel Boys, as the five members of Spandau Ballet became known, after the inner London district in which they grew up. Dagger knew everything there was to know about true Mods like Steve Marriott's Small Faces, who wore the sharpest skinny styles from Italy and had curtained hair with centre partings. At the time, Dagger was on a foundation course at St Martin's. His path soon crossed with Gary Kemp's moptop band who were playing Thrash and Power Pop, first as the Makers and then the Gentry. Dagger recognised that what they needed was a scene to align themselves with.

Life before personal computers is hard to imagine now, but in the 70s the latest technology was Space Invaders, ghetto-blasters and digital watches. The media amounted to three channels of TV offering two weekly Pop shows, plus the grown-up newspapers and four music weeklies. In 1980, the Daily Telegraph described Discos as a "dehumanising threat to civilisation."

Before the culture created at Blitz, there were no style gurus, like the Mod's "Faces", to propose what to wear. You dressed either as a Disco kid, a New Waver in black drains and narrow tie, or a Mohican wearing Punk. The Blitz Kids were the first children of the television age and they set out to control the areas they knew best: music and fashion. Gary Kemp said: "A cultural identity is a great outlet for people's frustrations. Kids have always spent what little they have on records and haircuts. They've never spent it on books by Karl Marx."

Although Steve Strange got the credit, Rich Kids drummer Rusty Egan was actually the founder of the club night at Blitz. He printed flyers declaring "fame fame fame" to lure Bowie outcasts to a tacky gay bar called Billy's, in Soho. In most of London's clubs, Tuesdays were a dead zone. "I'll fill it for you," said Egan. This was a pioneer for the principle of bar profits going to the club owner and door profits to the hosts. Egan enlisted his flatmate as door man, vetting the punters queuing at the door. Pop wannabe Steve Strange worked at a flouncy clothes shop called PX, which went on to establish the New Romantic look. The Blitz was decorated with a Second World War austerity that echoed the down-at-heel 70s: bare floorboards, gingham tablecloths, hanging lights with dusty enamel shades and framed pictures of Churchill. Its manager, Brendan Connolly, had been struggling to promote intimate cabaret, and the crowd attracted by Egan and Strange were cabaret incarnate.

The Blitz crowd distrusted anyone over 25. Chris Sullivan was a St Martin's fashion student, busy trying to reinvent the Zoot suit. He said at the time: "Young people are no longer prepared to be sold clothes they don't like or go to clubs playing records they don't want to hear, being run by grunters three times their age, and having to pay for the privilege."

When the Blitz opened, it was cheap, but it was also extraordinary to have someone aged 19 vetting the door. Spandau were the extra ingredient that pushed Blitz into its critical phase. Their mission was to return Pop to what Gary Kemp called a "visual extravaganza in the spirit of Ziggy Stardust".

Kemp had an intense dislike of the New Musical Express, or NME. Mere mention of the paper and its "stereotyped attitudes" had him fuming. Kemp said: "They don't understand style in working class terms: they think it means money. Well, it doesn't. One of the most difficult things is explaining what style is to middle class journalists because they always connect style with being bourgeois." This perception of antipathy is why Dagger refused to let most Rock journalists near his group throughout Spandau's first year. He knew that few of them had ever been inside a nightclub. "What's more, they can't dance," he'd snort. Before allowing access to Spandau, Dagger subjected all journalists to discreet vetting. Applicants wearing denim or Doc Martens never reached the shortlist.

Spandau Ballet had played only eight live gigs before they signed an unrivalled contract worth £300,000 in today's money. Only two record companies "got" what Spandau were about, CBS and Chrysalis. The second won by allowing the band greater creative freedom than was usual at the time. The band secured an unprecedented package: 14% against the normal rate of 8%. Their own record label, Reformation, retained management of publishing rights and merchandising. Chrysalis offered a promotional video and a 12-inch club mix with each single, which were firsts for a British band. The band agreed to a six-way split of the proceeds, with Dagger being de facto a member of the band. Two weeks after its release, their first single, *To Cut a Long Story Short*, entered the charts and reached No five. It was danceable, melodic and the vocalist could actually sing, which as cult sounds went, was unique. They called their new genre "White European Dance Music".

Within weeks of Spandau's hit, Britain's club grapevine propelled even more club land bands into the charts, many of them unveiled by sharp young managers the same age as their talent. 35 new look acts hit the charts during 1981 alone, including Visage, Ultravox, Duran Duran, the Human League, Heaven 17, Depeche Mode, Soft Cell, Toyah and ABC. This was one of the most fertile years for British Pop since the 60s. Nothing illustrated this better than two Top of the Pops Christmas shows, a year apart. As 1980 closed Spandau were the only act playing the new music. By Christmas 1981, TOTP had a sparkling neon-tech sett and a demented dance troupe called Zoo.

In 1978, London offered only one hip club night a week; by 1984 Time Out magazine listed 50, while the British Tourist Authority reported that dancing was a serious reason to visit the UK. London Transport put on a whole network of night buses.

To some, being young in the early 80s must have felt like heaven. British youth had what the world's Pop fans wanted. In America, twenty somethings craved groups of their own age. Britain's visual kaleidoscope of cults fed MTV from its launch in 1982 and loosened the stranglehold that music radio once held.

In 1983, Margaret Thatcher was re-elected and Britain enjoyed a consumer boom that lasted until 1985. Then along came Stock Aitken and Waterman, who made more than 100 UK top 40 hits and brought a return to the blandness of corporate brands.

Unlike many of Britain's youth cults, which were violently tribal, the New Romantics were not aggressive, although plenty of aggression was dished out to them by Punks and Skinheads. Their appearance attracted attention, as it ranged from androgynous to openly homosexual. Britain in the 1980s was a much less tolerant place than today and it had seen nothing like the New Romantics before. Looking back at old photographs of a Steve Strange and the other Blitz pioneers, they look very young and very much like victims in waiting.

Chapter 7.3
House Music and Ecstasy

House Music is a type of electronic music, which came as a direct development from the Saturday Night Fever style of Disco music. It was created by club DJs in Chicago in the early 1980s. Early House Music was characterised by repetitive rhythms produced by drum machines, with synthesised bass lines. House displayed some characteristics similar to the Disco music which preceded it. Both were dance music created by DJs, but House was more electronic and minimalistic. The repetitive rhythm of House became more important than the song itself; indeed, many House tracks were instrumental, with no vocals, or if there was singing, the singer would not be a well known artist.

House developed in Chicago's underground dance club culture during the early 1980s, as DJs from the gay subculture began altering the Disco dance tracks to give a mechanical beat and deeper basslines.

In the early 1980s, Chicago DJs, like Ron Hardy and Frankie Knuckles played many styles of dance music, including older Disco records. Some DJs made edits of their favourite songs on reel-to-reel tape recorders and sometimes mixed in electronic effects, drum machines, synthesisers and other rhythmic electronic instruments. The African American DJ Frankie Knuckles used basslines and rhythm sections from vintage Disco and R&B songs, mixed them with bits of modern synthpop songs and transformed them into new House Music tracks.

The term House Music is said to have originated in a Chicago club called The Warehouse, which traded between 1977 and 1983. Clubbers at The Warehouse were mostly black and came to dance to music played by Knuckles, who was the club's resident DJ. Fans referred to Knuckles as the "Godfather of House". Knuckles began the trend of splicing together different records when he found that most records were not long enough to satisfy his audience of dancers. In the Channel 4 documentary *Pump Up The Volume*, Knuckles remarked that the first time he saw the term "House Music" was on a sign saying "we play house music" in the window of a bar on Chicago's South Side. One of the people in the car with him joked, "you know, that's the kind of music you play down at the Warehouse."

In the mid-to-late 1980s, House Music crossed the Atlantic and became popular in Britain with songs like: *Pump Up The Volume* by MARRS (1987), *Theme from S'Express* by S'Express (1988) and *Doctorin' the House* by Coldcut (1988). The first House hit in the UK was Farley "Jackmaster" Funk's *Love Can't Turn Around*, which reached number 10 in the UK singles chart in September 1986. In January 1987, Chicago DJ Steve "Silk" Hurley's *Jack Your Body* reached number one in the UK, proving it was possible for House Music to achieve success in the Pop charts. Raze entered the top 20 in the same month with *Jack the Groove* and several other House hits reached the top ten that year.

After the number one success of *Pump Up The Volume,* British acts like The Beatmasters, Yazz, Bomb The Bass and S-Express also achieved UK chart success. Early British House Music quickly diversified from the original Chicago sound. Many of the early hits were based on sample montage and unlike the Americans' Soulful lyrics; Rap was often used for British vocals.

House was also being developed in the booming dance club scene in Ibiza. While no House artists or labels came from this holiday island, mixing experimentation by Ibiza DJs helped influence the British House style. By the mid-1980s a distinct Balearic mix of House had developed. Several influential clubs in Ibiza, like Amnesia, with DJ Alfredo at the decks, were playing a mix of Rock, Pop, Disco and house.

It was in Ibiza that the drug Ecstasy (MDMA), began to capture the House scene. Drugs had been a big part of the Northern Soul scene, but while they seem similar, the reason for their drug taking was very different. The Soul dancers used amphetamines to keep them going throughout their all night dances. But their minds were still in control of their actions. Ecstasy, however, completely took over its users, removing inhibitions and creating its own drug induced dance style.

By late 1987, DJs were bringing the Ibiza sound to British clubs like the Haçienda in Manchester. Ibiza influences also spread to London clubs like Shoom in Southwark, Heaven, Future and Spectrum. A new generation of clubs like Liverpool's Cream and the Ministry of Sound were opened to provide venues for more commercial House sounds.

One subgenre of House, Acid House, was based around the deep electronic tones created by Roland's TB-303 bass machine. It was also very heavily influenced by the Ecstasy taken by both performers and fans. "It's the closest thing to mass organised zombie-dom," said BBC Radio 1 DJ Peter Powell, when Acid House first arrived. "I really don't think it should go any further."

In the mid-80s, Britain's clubbers embraced Acid House, along with the new drug, Ecstasy. A new scene grew up around it that changed the social and cultural habits of an entire generation. Before Acid House, nightclubs in Britain were mostly places where people went to get drunk, meet someone of the opposite sex, or fight someone of the same sex. Acid House and Ecstasy turned nightclubs into places to dance.

One of the new Acid House Clubs was Manchester's Haçienda, which was opened by Factory Records on 21 May 1982. The Haçienda's name was from Ivan Chtcheglov's, "Formulary for a New Urbanism," which read: "You'll never see the haçienda, it doesn't exist. The haçienda must be built." Factory Records had not quite caight the mood of the time and had not considered who the Haçienda must be built for. In 1982, Manchester's scallies and students were not quite ready for a New York style Discotheque. "There wasn't anyone in the Haçi for the first five years; it was dead," remembered Happy Mondays' Shaun Ryder. "But it always felt like an important place where you knew things could happen." When Acid House arrived, the Haçienda vision finally made sense. The arrival of Ecstasy was all it took. "The summer of 1987 is when everything changed," remembered Ryder. "When life suddenly went from black and white to Technicolor. When we first got the E."

"At first, there were only about 15 of us at it, in our corner," said Eric Barker, a friend of Ryder's, "going bananas, dancing very weirdly, completely differently to everyone else, especially Bez. I'd always danced, but never with my hands in the air. Who did dance with their arms in the air before Ecstasy? No one in Manchester. But when the E arrived, all of a sudden you felt your hands rising up in the air. You couldn't help it."

Ecstasy also affected the clothes that people wore. In early 1988, there were still some people going to the Haçienda in suits with shoulder pads and then all of a sudden they started wearing dungarees.

During the summer of 1987 Paul Oakenfold was in Ibiza celebrating his 24th birthday, with: Johnny Walker, Danny Rampling and Nicky Holloway. Here, they encountered Ibiza DJ Alfredo, performing while under the influence of Ecstasy. They came home determined to recreate it in their own style. Oakenfold began playing House at his Project club, then he started Future and later Spectrum at Richard Branson's Heaven club. Rampling and his wife started Shoom, in a fitness centre at Southwark. Shoom was the first club to adopt the smiley logo that became synonymous with Acid House and its accompanying drug abuse.

At first, Ecstasy had the unexpected effect of calming down the hormone fuelled teenage violence. There was hardly any fighting between the clubbers, or other youth tribes. Even the most ultra violent of the youth cults, the Football Firms, became loved up through the drug. But violence returned when the unlicensed and illegal Rave parties began.

The violence was not directed towards any other youth cult, it was directed at the police. The Rave customers had two options: go home, or be arrested. They did not want either of them. Unfortunately, this led to violent encounters over option three. The dancers insisted on being left to party, but to maintain the rule of law, the police had to enforce the first two options, by force if necessary.

The Blackburn Raves began in 1989. The first few were very small events for friends, but as their reputation grew they started attracting people from Manchester, Leeds, Liverpool and further afield. "Traffic was converging from all over," remembered Drew Hemment, who DJ'd at the later Raves. The biggest fun of the night was the chase, trying to find the warehouse while evading the police.

Manchester Acid House group Together met at a Blackburn Rave and later returned to record crowd noise for their track *Hardcore Uproar*. "Just after we finished recording," remembered Suddi Raval, "police raided it and started beating people." The big large Blackburn Rave, held in 1990, attracted 10,000 people to its venue at Nelson, near Burnley. This was also raided by police. "It started to get heavy. A police car was turned over, another one was torched," says Hemment. "At 7am the police marched in, banging their shields. Some of the crowd managed to get the back door open and people poured out."

In August 1988, Tony Colston-Hayter hosted the first of the big commercial warehouse Raves at Wembley Studios in London, under the name Apocalypse Now. Many hard core fans consider this to be Acid House's tipping point. Colston-Hayter let ITN film the event, the first time news cameras had been let into a Rave. Some of the early Acid House devotees, especially those from Shoom and Spectrum, thought this new type of commercial promoter was diluting what they had built. "That's when it exploded," said Mark Moore of S'Express. " Apocalypse Now told everyone they'd invited film crews down and Jenni Rampling was saying, 'Do not be part of this.' But I went anyway. When the programme went out, it wasn't showing what a wonderful scene it was; it was shock-horror coverage like, 'Your children are all on drugs!' That's when it changed and all the shock tabloid headlines came out. It was a wonderful, beautiful period before that, but it was inevitable: there was no way we were going to be able to keep a lid on this thing."
"I didn't go to any of those big raves," said Andrew Weatherall. "They just seemed too commercial. But now, when I see the films, I sometimes wish I hadn't been quite so purist because some of them look great. What really strikes me is how multi-racial they were."
The press thought differently of Colston-Hayter, and dubbed him "the Acid House King" and "Acid's Mr Big". He changed the name of his events to Sunrise, hired a young PR man called Paul Staines, who later became the political blogger Guido Fawkes. Colston-Hayter was unapologetic about turning Rave into a commercial

enterprise, saying: "Maggie should be proud of us: we're a product of enterprise culture."

Following hard on the heels of Apocalypse Now came a series of huge, often outdoor Raves, including Sunrise, Biology, Genesis and many others, including those around the new M25 London orbital motorway, from which the band Orbital took their name. Jarvis Cocker later sang about one of the Raves in Pulp's *Sorted for Es and Wizz:* "Oh, is this the way they say the future's meant to feel? Or just 20,000 people standing in a field."

While the media sensationalised the dangers of Acid House and Ecstasy, the movement itself became a challenge to authority, prompting parliament to pass new legislation. The police also established a unit dedicated to disrupting unlicensed parties. A movement that had been pro-hedonism became political and anti-authority by default. The Criminal Justice and Public Order Act 1994 was passed to ban large Rave events featuring music with "repetitive beats." It was passed mainly due to police evidence that the events were closely linked to illegal club drugs. There were several "Kill the Bill" demonstrations by Rave and electronic dance music fans.

The Spiral Tribe event at Castle Morten was the last of the illegal Raves, as the bill, which became law, in November 1994, made the events illegal in the UK.

There is another sub-culture that developed as an unlikely spin off from the Rave scene. This was the partnering up of hedonistic clubbers, with the more Hippy like, New Age Travellers. The Travellers saw the Raves as a reincarnation of the Free Festivals and they began to include the underground Rave events into their travels. But this happened in the 1990s, so I will discuss them further in that decade.

Chapter 7.4
Goth

Goth was another sub culture that had its roots in England, not America. Compared to many other youth cults, it has been a fairly long lasting culture, beginning in the early 1980s and possibly becoming even stronger today. There will be few people who cannot visualise the Goths' black clothing, dyed black hair, dark eyeliner, black fingernails and black period styled clothing. But Goth is much deeper than just a fashion attached to a music genre, although in common with all of the youth cults, it does have a musical accompaniment. Its musical history comes from Gothic Rock, itself an offshoot of the post Punk age. Notable post Punk groups that pre-dated the emergence of Goth include Siouxsie and the Banshees, Joy Division and Bauhaus. The Goth subculture survived much longer than other cultures of the same era and continued to diversify as it spread throughout the world. Its imagery has strong influences from 19th century Gothic literature and Gothic horror films.

The term "Gothic Rock" was first used in 1967 by music critic John Stickney. He was describing a meeting he had with Jim Morrison in a dimly lit wine-cellar which he called "the perfect room to honour the Gothic Rock of the Doors".

By the late 70s, the "Gothic" adjective was being used to describe post-Punk bands like Siouxsie and the Banshees and Joy Division. In a review of a Siouxsie and the Banshees' concert in July 1978, critic Nick Kent wrote that, "parallels and comparisons can now be drawn with Gothic Rock architects like the Doors." Later that year, the term was repeated by Joy Division's manager, Tony Wilson in an interview for the BBC. Wilson described Joy Division as "Gothic" compared to the Pop mainstream. The name was later applied to newer bands like Bauhaus who followed in the wake of Joy Division and Siouxsie and the Banshees. Bauhaus's first single, in 1979, *Bela Lugosi's Dead*, is often credited as being the starting point of the Gothic Rock genre.

In 1979, *Sounds* magazine described Joy Division as "Gothic" and "theatrical". In February 1980, *Melody Maker* called them "masters of this Gothic gloom".

But, it was not until the early 80s that Gothic Rock became a distinct music subgenre, with followers who came together as a distinctly recognisable movement. The "Goth" mantle was also popularised in a 1981 article published in the British Rock weekly *Sounds*: "The face of Punk Gothique", written by Steve Keaton. In his article Keaton asked: "Could this be the coming of Punk Gothique? In July 1982, the opening of the Batcave in Soho provided a meeting point for London Goths.

The bands who defined the Gothic Rock genre included Bauhaus, early Adam and the Ants, the Cure, Southern Death Cult, Sex Gang Children, UK Decay, Virgin Prunes, Killing Joke, and the Damned.

The Goth culture of the 80s drew its inspiration from several sources. Some of them were modern or contemporary; others were centuries-old. Among the music subcultures that influenced Goth were Punk, New Wave and Glam. But it also drew inspiration from Gothic literature, horror films, vampire cults, science fiction film noirs, like Ridley Scott's *Blade Runner*, and traditional mythology. Notable Goth icons include: Siouxsie Sioux of the Banshees, Robert Smith of The Cure, Peter Murphy of Bauhaus, Rozz Williams of Christian Death, Ian Curtis of Joy Division, and Dave Vanian of The Damned.

Some of the early Gothic Rock artists adopted horror film images and drew on horror film soundtracks for inspiration. Some members of Bauhaus were themselves, art students or active artists. Their audiences responded by adopting dress and props to mirror the image being created for them. Horror film props like swirling smoke, rubber bats, and cobwebs often featured as gothic club décor from their beginning in Soho's Batcave.

In the beginning, such references by the bands in their music and image were tongue-in-cheek, but as time went on, the subculture took the connection more seriously. As a result, morbid and occult themes became more noticeable in the subculture. The connection between horror and Goth was highlighted in *The Hunger*, a 1983 vampire film starring David Bowie, Catherine Deneuve and Susan Sarandon. The film featured Bauhaus performing *Bela Lugosi's Dead* in a nightclub.

As the subculture became established, the connection between Goth and horror fiction became almost a cliché, with Goths often appearing as characters in horror films. For example, *The Craft, The*

Crow, The Matrix and Underworld film series drew their style directly from Goth.

The two annual highlights for English Goths are the Whitby Goth Weekends. They are alternative music festivals held in the North Yorkshire seaside town. The events have two nights of live bands, three days of alternative trade stalls and a custom car & bike show. The festival's origin is from a meeting of about 40 Goth pen pals in 1994. Their first meeting was in the Elsinore pub in Whitby which, with the Little Angel continues to be a meeting point for Goths during the festivals.

Whitby was chosen for its Dracula connections. The festival was held once a year until 1997, after which it became a twice yearly event, in April and October. It has grown into one of the world's most popular Goth events attracting about 1,500 people. The main event is hosted at the town's largest venue Whitby Spa Pavilion. The Spa is also one of three sites for the Bizarre Bazaar 'Goth Market' along with Whitby Leisure Centre and the Brunswick Centre.

The "weekend" officially starts on Friday, although fringe events are held on Thursday, Sunday and Monday. Festival Events include club nights, markets, and a charity football match between a visiting Goth team called Real Gothic and local team Stokoemotiv Whitby. During the October event there is also a custom car show, 'Whitby Kustom' held in the grounds of West Cliff School.

The event means booming business for the town, with the two weekends contributing £1.1 million each year to the local economy. During the mid-2000s the October weekend, which is held close to

Halloween started attracting lots of non-Goths in Halloween, horror, historical and Sci-Fi costume, which led to a big increase in visitors and photographers. The weekends now also attract other alternative cultures, including Victorian vampires, Rockers, Punks and Steam Punk enthusiasts.

Far from the usually wild image of teenage cults, the Goths have a better reputation. The BBC reported on academic research that portrayed Goths as "refined and sensitive, keen on poetry and books, not big on drugs or anti-social behaviour." The researchers also found that teens often remained in the subculture well into adult life and were likely to become well educated.

Where there has been violence involving Goths, it has generally been directed towards them, as punishment for being odd, or different. Goths sometimes suffer prejudice and discrimination, with outsiders sometimes marginalising Goths, either by intention or by accident. Actress Christina Hendricks talked about being bullied when she was a Goth in school and how difficult it was for her to deal with peer pressure: "Kids can be pretty judgmental about people who are different. But instead of breaking down and conforming, I stood firm. That is also probably why I was unhappy. My mother was mortified and kept telling me how horrible and ugly I looked. Strangers would walk by with a look of shock on their face, so I never felt pretty. I just always felt awkward". Prejudice will often move people into circles of bonding, where they can share similar experiences and be accepted. This in turn strengthens the bonds of the culture.

Probably Britain's worst example of violence towards Goths occurred on 11th August 2007, when a young couple walking through Stubbylee Park in Lancashire, were attacked by a gang of teenagers because they were Goths. Sophie Lancaster later died from her injuries. Two teenagers, Ryan Herbert and Brendan Harris, were convicted of murdering of Sophie and were given life sentences. Three others were given lesser sentences assaulting her boyfriend Robert Maltby. In delivering his sentence, Judge Anthony Russell said, "This was a hate crime against these completely harmless people targeted because their appearance was different to yours". He went on to defend the Goth community, calling Goths "perfectly peaceful, law-abiding people who pose no threat to anybody".

While walking home, Sophie and Anthony were subjected to a mob attack. It happened around 1am at the skate park area of Stubbylee Park. The couple came across a gang of teenagers at the entrance to the park. The gang followed them and assaulted Anthony, knocking him unconscious and then set upon Sophie, who was shielding her boyfriend. A witness told police: "They were running over and just kicking her in the head and jumping up and down on her head". One witness used a mobile phone to call for emergency services saying: "We need... we need an ambulance at Bacup Park, this Mosher has just been banged because he's a Mosher". Witnesses said that afterwards, "The killers boasted about their attack on the Goths, or "Moshers," by telling friends afterwards that they had "done summat good," and claiming: "There's two Moshers nearly dead up Bacup park, you wanna see them, they're a right mess".

Police said that it was "a sustained attack during which the pair received serious head injuries and their faces were so swollen we could not ascertain which one was female and which one was male". Both were hospitalised as a result of the attack. Anthony's injuries left him in a coma and with internal bleeding. He gradually recovered, but lost memory of the time leading up to and during, the attack.

Sophie was in a deep coma and was placed on life support. The doctors determined that she would never regain consciousness and her life support was terminated.

In 2013, police in Manchester announced they would be treating attacks on members of alternative subcultures, like Goths, in the same way that they treat attacks based on race, religion, and sexual orientation.

Part 8 - the 1990s

Chapter 8.1
Illegal Raves

A Rave, or Free Party, as they are also called, is a party "free" from the restrictions of the regulated club scene; it usually involves a sound system playing electronic dance music from late at night until such time as the organisers decide to go home. The parties are considered autonomous zones where the people themselves make and enforce the rules. This typically means that drugs are freely available and noise levels are illegally high.

Drug dealing and misuse is long embedded within the Rave culture. Most commonly used are MDMA (Ecstasy), Cocaine, LSD, Cannabis, Nitrous Oxide (laughing gas) and Ketamine. Drugs are easily available at almost all free parties, with people often using them to reduce the fatigue of from dancing for many hours, as well as their recreational effects.

In early years Ecstasy was the most common drug taken at parties, however over recent years there has been a steady increase in the use of Ketamine. Some party goers have said that the massive presence of Ketamine spoiled the atmosphere found at earlier parties.

After the emergence of the Acid House parties in the late 80s Raves were attracting up to 4,000 people. These events happened almost every weekend. The noise and disturbance caused by thousands of people attending parties in rural locations caused outrage in the media.

After sensational coverage in the tabloids and a particularly large rave at Castlemorton in May 1992, the government acted on what was seen as a growing menace. In 1994, the Criminal Justice Bill was passed into law as the Criminal Justice and Public Order Act 1994. This Act contained sections designed to suppress both Raves and the growing anti road protest movement.

The newly set fine for running an illegal party was £20,000, or six months in prison and police crackdowns drove the Rave scene into the countryside. The word "Rave" became used to describe semi spontaneous parties occurring at locations just outside the M25, that attracted up to 25 000 people.

Under the Criminal Justice and Public Order Act 1994, the definition of music played at a rave was: "music" includes sounds wholly or predominantly characterised by the emission of a succession of repetitive beats.

The number of people attending such an event for it to be illegal was later reduced by the Anti-social Behaviour Act 2003. The law now covers indoor and outdoor parties with more than 20 people attending.

Castlemorton Common was the event that led to these strict new laws being passed. On a hot bank holiday weekend in 1992, 20,000 people descended on land near the Malvern Hills. Word about the event was spread by an answering machine message: "Right, listen up revellers. It's happening now and for the rest of the weekend, so get yourself out of the house and on to Castlemorton Common... Be there, all weekend, hardcore."

Carl Loben wrote in DJ magazine, that, in a world before mobile phones, answering machine messages were key to spreading word about the Raves. "There was often just a message left that people could call in the evening. It would say the Rave is at [some location], meet at [this] junction of the motorway, or meet in the service station, and you'd go in convoy."

What began as a small free festival for Travellers went down in history as the biggest illegal Rave ever held in Britain. But it also resulted in a trial costing £4m and the passing of the Criminal Justice and Public Order Act.

The publicity resulting from Castlemorton Common also had drastic consequences for the "alternative" lifestyle of the New Age Travellers who created the event and for the underground Rave movement who gate crashed it.

The travellers had been intent on holding the latest in a series of small events. They had successfully run the Avon Free Festival at Inglestone Common in Gloucestershire during the 1980s and early 90s. In the weeks leading up to the 1992 May bank holiday, they had tried and failed to stage festivals in Avon, Gloucestershire and Somerset, where the police had repeatedly moved them on.

In retreat, they considered their options in a Gloucestershire lay-by on the A38, where they decided to take their 10 mile long convoy into Worcestershire and on to the 392 acre Castlemorton Common, which was made a Site of Special Scientific Interest in 1986.

Libby Spragg was one of the first Travellers to arrive on the 22nd May. She spoke to the BBC about her experience. The 24 year old joined the New Age Travellers in 1987 and had been to several previous events across the West Country, including Inglestone. She said the festivals were a chance "for networking, finding new work opportunities and just meeting friends that you couldn't really see at any other time", after a winter spent working on farms.

"Ingleston Common had one small stage, no dance music and was part of the small free festival scene that had been bubbling along since the 60s." Castlemorton was meant to continue that theme, she said, a low-key gathering for about 400 Travellers.

What they hadn't banked on was the thousands of people who heard about the event through word-of-mouth, media coverage and the infamous answering machine message.

Then the underground warehouse Rave scene arrived, with its big sound systems in tow. Libby said there was "some resentment" among the Travellers who felt their event had been "taken over" and part of the festival was declared a "Raver free zone".

But it was not just the Travellers who felt surrounded, so did people living around the common, like Mary Weaver. "On the bank below the hills it was tightly compacted and as you went down by our pond there were double decker buses lined up all along there," she remembered. "It was very disruptive because no-one could get in or out with a vehicle." "They had some very loud sound systems and they played very loud music, but in actual fact the music didn't worry me that much, because I like music. But it did bother other people, it drove them mad. It stopped about five o'clock in the morning and it started up about midday."

News of the festival spread locally, helped by the volume of the music, which could easily be heard 10 miles away in Malvern. A fact to which former resident, Tim Holloway, attested. "I was coming back from an all night party in Malvern and walking back at about five in the morning I could hear this booming beat. I had no idea what it could be," he said. "Later someone told me there was this massive rave on Castlemorton Common." "We rode through on motorbikes and I was stunned, it was just enormous. We took it all in, soaked up the atmosphere. It was just an enormous party; a gift to a 21 year old."

Clare Buchanan heard about the festival when Travellers en route stopped at the supermarket in Malvern where she worked. "They looked like full-on hippies, which is what I wanted to be," she recalled. "Me and a friend went along to investigate what was going on. We were dropped off and there were two policemen at the end of the road across the common. There was a very chilled atmosphere."

By Saturday night, West Mercia Police had arrived and erected a cordon. Officers were stationed with Ms Weaver and fellow resident Audrey Street who said that she "never went out once" the whole week. She described how the single track road across the common was completely blocked in places by the camp and the absence of toilets had another unsavoury effect. "Every time I went out there were people in the field toileting. Every time you looked out there were men with their trousers down," she said. The encampment stretched up the hill from the farm near her house

The Ravers drifted off once the weekend was over but the Travellers remained at Castlemorton until the Friday, partly to try and clear up. Libby Spragg claimed; "I think a lot of people were depressed about the mess and the waste, that's why so many of us stayed behind and tried to clear up." Although people don't think it, the Traveller ethos at free festivals was "leave no trace; you went there, you had a party you cleaned up." "In fact I was one of the many people who used to take wild flower seeds, and that would be the only thing I left - that sounds like I'm a real Hippy but that was the vibe," she said.

The fallout of the festival had a lasting impact on the travelling scene. In a press conference on the Friday after the event, then Chief Constable, David Blakey, defended his "softly softly" approach. "Faced with... the number of people that were there, there was no way I'm going in with riot shields, with public order gear, to move them off," he said at the time.

Officers arrested about 50 people during the festival, mainly for drug offences and 10 were charged with public order offences. The case cost millions and resulted in all the defendants being acquitted. The force later admitted they had been "caught off guard" by the sudden arrival of so many people.

Determined not to let history repeat itself, the following year they set up roadblocks across the area, with 300 officers, who were fed from a special kitchen set up in the village hall.

The Malvern Hills Conservators, a charity set up to look after the hills and commons, obtained an injunction which enforced a five mile "exclusion zone" for convoys of vehicles around Castlemorton during the bank holiday weekend.

Then in 1994, the Criminal Justice and Public Order Act was passed, giving police the powers to stop vehicles anywhere within five miles of a Rave and turn them away. It also included rules targeting gatherings of more than 100 people listening to music at night.

Libby Spragg, who gave up travelling in 1995, said that what happened at Castlemorton had an adverse effect on the community she belonged to. "The travelling scene did carry on but it was a very different change of lifestyle for people. They moved onto farms instead of living on free sites and people were a lot more scared."

Despite the new laws, free parties continued to exist. In August 2006, an unlicensed party in Essex was broken up after 24 hours resulting in 60 injuries on both sides and over 50 arrests. This was one of the largest confrontations at an unlicensed event for many years. The Chief Superintendent in charge of the police operation said "These sorts of Raves are quite unheard of in this county. I have not seen this sort of violence since the old days of acid house."

Chapter 8.2
Britain's Rap

By the 1990s, Rap was very much entrenched in British youth culture. But it had changed from the benign form of street culture that developed in New York during the 70s. In Jamaica there was violence ingrained in the culture, where Rude Boy heavies either protected, or disrupted rival performances. Once adapted to the American streets, Hip Hop became something of an alternative to violence, with gang members holding Rap and Breakdance contests. But the version we inherited in Britain was the violent avaristic Gangsta Rap version, which has often been condemned for glorifying guns, drugs and violence.

British Hip Hop was originally influenced by the style of dub / toasting introduced by Jamaican migrants in the 1960s and 70s, who eventually developed rapping, or speed-toasting, in order to match the rhythm of the ever increasing pace of Jamaican-influenced dub.

Just as it had done in America, British Hip Hop developed as an off shoot from graffiti and breakdancing, then moving through to DJing and live rapping at parties and club nights. Initially, its supporters listened to and were influenced by American Hip Hop. Unlike in America, the British scene was always cross-racial. This is because various ethnic groups in Britain tended not to live in segregated areas. This allowed youths to share a cultural interchange with each another's musical genres, as we saw in the early days of the Skinheads. Cross pollination through migrating West Indians helped to develop a community interested in the music. The introduction of powerful sound systems brought a distinct British Caribbean influence.

The first British Hip Hop tune released on record is credited as; *Christmas Rapping*, by Dizzy Heights in 1982. There were earlier Pop records which dabbled with rap, such as: Adam and the Ants' *Ant Rap* in 1981 and Wham's *Wham Rap* in 1982, but these were usually considered Pop adaptations of American rap.

Sex Pistols' manager Malcolm McLaren produced *Buffalo Gals*, in 1982, featuring the New York Hip Hop group World's Famous Supreme Team. This is generally thought of as the breakthrough hit that introduced Hip Hop to Britain.

In the early days, a lack of radio play and publicity prevented the fledgling scene from growing and Hip Hop only survived through the patronage of pirate radio stations. Mainstream radio did occasionally play British Hip Hop, through the patronage of DJs such as John Peel and Tim Westwood, a white British DJ who affected a ridiculous fake Jamaican accent.

Tim Westwood is the middle-class son of a former Bishop of Peterborough. He joined Radio 1 in 1994 to present the station's first dedicated Rap show. Westwood was often mocked for speaking in the street slang of the black Rap artists he championed. The DJ was believed to have inspired Sacha Baron Cohen's comic creation

Ali G, who satirised white Rap fans' attempts to copy the style and speech patterns of black culture.

I met Westwood in 2005, when I policed his event at a Nottingham night club. Already 42, he was considerably older than his audience and appeared a very cartoon like character, with his jewellery, tracksuit and customised American van.

Despite the ridicule, the Sony Award winning broadcaster introduced several generations of listeners to Hip Hop and helped a wave of British performers achieve success in the US dominated genre. He has more than 400,000 Twitter followers and his YouTube channel has received more than 180 million views.

Westwood hit the headlines when he was injured in a drive-by shooting in South London in 1999. Gunmen on a motorbike reportedly pulled up alongside his Range Rover and shot him and his assistant.

His show was accused of playing tracks which promoted knife violence by David Cameron in a 2006 speech, a claim Radio 1 fiercely disputed.

Westwood outlasted many of his contemporaries on Radio 1. He lasted until 2013, when aged 55, the BBC axed his show after nearly 20 years as Radio 1's voice of Rap. He was replaced by rising star Charlie Sloth, in a shake-up designed to promote a new generation of "urban" presenters. Radio 1 was trying to reduce the average age of its listeners from 29 and was prepared to lose long standing presenters to appeal to a younger audience.

British Hip Hop in the 1980s was not just confined to music and break dancing, it also involved New York style graffiti; another integral element of American Hip Hop culture. The most direct influence was the graffiti painted on London Underground trains. Just when Subway graffiti was declining in New York, some British teenagers who had spent time in Queens and the Bronx returned to London with a mission to Americanise the London Underground through painting New York graffiti on our trains.

A new generation of artists emerged after the turn of the century, performing a new style of electronic music, influenced by, Garage, Dancehall and Drum and Bass. The new genre was called Grime and quickly superseded Hip Hop in popularity. The mid 2000s saw controversy about the lyrical content in Grime music. Records such as *Pow*! in 2005, by Lethal Bizzle made numerous references to guns and were banned from receiving air play.

The embrace of Gangster style of Hip Hop brought about criticism from politicians like David Blunkett, who said that British Hip Hop perpetuated violence.

Road Rap, also known as British Gangsta Rap, emerged as a backlash against the commercialisation of Grime in the late. Road Rap kept the explicit depictions of violence and gang culture found in early Grime music, while combining it with a style more similar to American Gangsta Rap. The Road Rap scene centred around mixtape releases and YouTube videos with some of the more popular acts even getting mainstream recognition. The genre has been criticised for the violence in its lyrics as well as its links to gangs and gun crime, with many rappers having served prison sentences.

In similar with Grime, Road Rap suffered from pre emptive policing with artists claiming that the Metropolitan Police set out to prevent them from making a living, by banning them from touring. Many new Trap and Drill crews were affiliated with gangs and most were being watched by the police, because of the violent themes in their music. London Drill is a subgenre of Drill music that came from Brixton in the early 2010s. Borrowing heavily from Chicago Drill music, London Drill artists rapped about a violent and hedonistic criminal lifestyle. Typically, those that created this style of music were affiliated with gangs or came from neighbourhoods where crime was a way of life. London Drill music is also related to Road Rap, a British style of Gangsta Rap. London Drill became popular due to its violent language and fierce Gang rivalries associated with it. Many of these artists took influences from the American Trap scene and added a British sound and flavour to the genre. The Chicago born Drill style of Rap has arguably been one of the most criticised forms of Rap. Its lyrics are often vivid accounts of taking drugs and violence. The videos made to accompany the music brought condemnation from Metropolitan Police Commissioner Cressida Dick, who blamed the videos for fuelling London's surge in murders and violent crime. She asked YouTube to delete videos which glamorised violence. Mike West, also from the Metropolitan Police, added "The gangs try to outrival each other with their filming and content. What looks like a music video often contains explicit language with gangs threatening each other. There are gestures of violence, with hand signals suggesting they are firing weapons and graphic descriptions of what they would do to each other.

YouTube seems to agree with the Police, as their spokesman said they had deleted more than half of the "violent" music videos that the Commissioner asked it to remove. The YouTube spokesman said: "We have developed policies specifically to tackle videos related to knife crime and are continuing to work constructively with experts on this issue. We share the deep concern about this issue and do not want our platform used to incite violence."

In February 2018, 17 year-old rapper Junior Simpson was sentenced to life in prison after he and three friends stabbed 15 year old Jermaine Goupall to death. The court heard he had written a track about knife attacks before committing the murder. Giving him a life sentence, Judge Leonard QC told Simpson: "You suggested your lyrics were just for show but I do not believe that, and I suspect you were waiting for the opportunity for an attack."

Over the last two years police asked YouTube to take down more than 50 music videos, because they were thought to incite violence. The Drill artists are pushing back. Pressplay, a company that promotes Drill videos, said on its Instagram page that police had "forced" YouTube to take some clips due to what's happened in London lately. A group of Drill artists called 1011 also launched an online petition to try and stop YouTube from taking down its videos.

Evidence from defendant Junior Andrews for the shooting of St Ann's teenager Danielle Beccan gave a clear description of Nottingham's culture of guns, drugs and gangs. His evidence also showed clear links between Nottingham's gang culture and Gangsta Rap. Andrews removed his shirt during the trial, to show the jury his gang tattoos. He was a fan of American Rapper Tupac and had the same tattoo on his arms as his idol wore on his stomach; "Thug Life". Asked what it meant, he said: "It means hard time, hard life. I've had a hard time, hard life." He also showed jurors a tattoo "NG2" on his neck, which is the postcode for The Meadows. On his right upper arm, he has a revolver and the initials "WFG", standing for "The Waterfront Gang".

Andrews was asked to explain the lyrics of music he was seen rapping on a video, including the phrases, "my water killers, my NG2 killers" and "going to St Ann's on a little creep, looking for my enemies", he insisted it was not "for real". He told the court: "It's just music at the end of the day. That's what music is... A big part of the music from America is based on gang warfare. Everyone knows that there's gang warfare going on in Nottingham and we're just reflecting it." Andrews told the jury that one of his friends had been shot in the leg and that another had been crippled by a beating, carried out by people from St Ann's.

BBC News interviewed people in the communities of St Ann's and The Meadows and one said: "It is like the Wild West... it is a war zone."

Speaking about people from St Ann's, one Meadows teenager said: "They are like aliens to me. It is massive, because of all the hate and guns that happen."

Another youth said: "It is big to be a gunman. Put a real gun in a 13 or 14 year old's hands and it is like a magnet. The majority of young people I know have access to a gun. If they have a 'beef' the first thing they do is shoot."

Chapter 8.3
Shottingham

I spent close to 25 years policing Nottinghamshire, where, at its worst, the Gangsta culture led to the city being called Shottingham. As described above in the trial of Junior Andrews, there are clear links between Gangsta Rap and the culture of violence on inner city estates. But the origins of gang crime in Nottingham date back several decades. Writer Carl Felstrom conducted an excellent piece of investigative journalism in his book; *Hoods, the Gang's of Nottingham*. He traced the roots of Nottingham's gangs back to the 1950s. After WWII, many immigrants saw Britain as a chance to throw off the restraints of the old world and start a new life in a new country. With Britain unprepared for integration, tension between the white working class and the Caribbean immigrants led to an outbreak of violence in the St Anns area during August 1958. Over two weekends, 4,000 men took part in street battles around Wells Road and Robin Hood Chase. After the riots, public housing policy changed and many immigrants were moved into Hyson Green, St Ann's and The Meadows.

Into this smoking cauldron arrived Vincent and Wellesley Robinson, in the early 1960s. Their family would become infamous in Nottingham.

Vincent; who became known as PG Man, was 20, while Wellesley; known as Douggie Man, was 22. PG Man and Douggie Man soon began running regular Blues nights at their homes in Nottingham and with Cannabis freely available, it was a sure bet that they would be raided by police sooner or later.

PG Man had spent three months in prison during the early 1960s after being caught with Cannabis. Douggie Man was also arrested for Cannabis possession in August 1966.

But things would become much worse: PG Man started working for the police. They had told him that he would be allowed to run his shebeen, sell Cannabis and stay out of prison if he informed on his friends and family. In the end, even PG's brother Douggie Man was arrested as a result of information given to the police. He faced a three year prison sentence and it became obvious to everyone that PG Man was working for the police. By now he had acquired another nickname: 'Judas'.

By the late 1970s and early 1980s, many younger members of the community were involved in crime. The Rude Boys of the second generation were of a rougher character than their fathers. Some had begun carrying knives and guns, robbing people and pimping prostitutes. Then Crack Cocaine reached the estates. By 1989, police had started to see the symptoms of this new Cocaine derivative in Radford, St Anns and The Meadows.

Even before Crack began to appear, Jamaican criminals on the run from the authorities back home would regularly lie low in Nottingham, with a distant relative or friend. But now with the growth of Crack Cocaine use, many more of the violent Jamaican gangsters known as Yardies were appearing in Nottingham. They hung around the Black and White Café in Radford Road and the Marcus Garvey Centre, in Lenton Boulevard. They swaggered around wearing heavy gold chains, selling rocks of Crack at a late night bar in Ilkeston Road, the Tally Ho; which was later called the Lenton, then the Drum.

In the early 1990s younger members of the St Anns community, now known in ghetto terms as the Stanz, formed a gang and called themselves the Playboy Posse. They soon got into a war with the Meadows Posse, who would later become known as the Waterfront Gang. It was the start of the black-on-black gang violence that was to blight the city for the next 15 years. No one knows exactly how it all started, but by the early 1990s, gang life within St Anns and The Meadows estates was flourishing. In late 1999, the number of shootings taking place in Nottingham began to rise dramatically. By November 2001, Operation Real Estate, in which armed police patrolled the streets, had made 400 arrests and recovered more than 100 firearms. 47 Jamaican nationals were among those arrested.

But gun crime continued to rise and the police decided a new approach was needed. In July 2002 they set up Operation Stealth to tackle black-on-black shootings by arresting offenders with firearms before they committed serious crimes. But the murders and shootings were still taking place. Two murders, committed soon after the launch of Operation Stealth, had the fingerprints of Yardie gunmen on them. On November 9, 2002, 33 year old Theresa Jacobs, a Crack Cocaine dealer, was shot in the head outside the Drum nightclub. Almost a year later on November 7, 2003, 24 year old Omar Watson visited his local barber shop to have his hair cut, but as he sat in his chair a gunman walked in and shot him dead.

By far the most publicised of Nottingham's shootings was the 2005 murder of 14 year old Danielle Beccan. The subsequent trial and conviction of Junior Andrews proved this resulted from the gang feud between St Anns and The Meadows. But, it is also yet another example of where media spin has not told a completely accurate story. The shooting of a 14 year old cannot be described as anything other than unacceptable, but while the media played hard on Junior Andrews' gang connections, they painted Danielle as an innocent young girl, who had nothing to do with the gangs. There is no evidence to suggest she was an active criminal, but many of the people she mixed with were deeply entrenched in St Anns' gang culture.

The headlines all ran with the theme that 14 year old Danielle was returning from an evening out with a group of friends at Nottingham's medieval Goose Fair when she was shot. While this is mostly accurate, there are certain facts missing from the headlines. October 9th 2005 was a Sunday evening, meaning that the 14 year old and any friends of her own age would have had school the next morning. Yet the ambulance was called shortly after 12.30 am. This was three and a half hours after the 9 pm closing of the Goose Fair on a Sunday evening. Neither did the media accurately report the ages and gang connections of some of Danielle's friends. While Danielle's murder was undoubtedly tragic, its portrayal in the media did nothing to discourage youngsters from their associations with the gangs.

Junior Andrews, 23, and Mark Kelly, 20, killed Danielle as part of a feud between gangs from the St Anns and Meadows areas of Nottingham. They were members of the Waterfront gang and attacked Danielle and her friends because they were in St Anns and associates of the Stanz Gangstas.

A witness at the trial, said "Everyone was laughing and joking as we walked back from the fair. There were four boys with us. I saw a gold car drive past, but I didn't think anything of it. When we got to Rushworth Close the car was already there and I could see that it had tinted windows. The lights then came on, the windows went down. Then I saw a hand in a black glove come out and point directly at us. I heard two shots but they didn't sound real at first and I thought it was a cap gun. Everyone screamed and ran but I didn't know where to go so I hid behind a tree. Then I saw Danielle lying there."

At least six bullets were fired and Danielle was hit once in the stomach. She collapsed to the ground and died later, in hospital.

Superintendent David Colbeck said they had received intelligence that there might be trouble at the fair, and measures had been put in place, but the information was not specific and the measures did not include additional patrols in St Anns, where Danielle lived and was shot. He added: "We still have a long long way to go. There is still a core of individuals who believe the only way they can build their business is by using firearms."

Detective Superintendant Kevin Flint, who led the investigation, said the case had been hampered by fear and intimidation because of the gang element.

It was the latest in a series of gun related incidents which plagued Nottingham at the time. Experts feared the city had become infested with "super thugs" who ordered minions to do their bidding while earning millions of pounds from narcotics. Jamaican Yardies, many of whom repeatedly thwarted deportation attempts, also had a strong foothold in the city's Heroin and Crack Cocaine market. Nottinghamshire's Chief Constable at the time was Steve Green. He was a vociferous critic of liberal justice values and described his force as being swamped by gun and drug crime. Following the shooting, he opened a wider debate about the criminal justice system, saying that society's emphasis on tolerance and understanding was a "failed" social experiment. He said "The evidence was on the streets, where youngsters behaved badly but knew how to play the system."

Some good did come out of Danielle's murder, through a trust fund which sought a return to Hip Hop's more innocent days. A memorial trust was set up in Danielle's name and ten years after her murder it had given out £300,000 to projects in and around the city. Nina Dauban, Chief Executive of the Nottinghamshire Community Foundation which administers the fund, said: "It's wonderful to see that in spite of tragedy, it can turn to something of huge benefit to local young people." She added that her legacy is living on in projects that contribute to the "love of the arts in young people like Danielle". The fund gives out awards of £30,000 each year to local charities and community projects under the theme of creative arts, including community choirs, a steel band for the Blue Mountain Women's Group and community recording studios. Mapperley Park based musical training group Magdala is also among those to have been supported from the fund.

In a candid interview with the Nottingham Post in 2016, Nathan Kelly spoke about how he got involved with the city's gang culture and why he eventually turned his back on it. Nathan was involved with gangs by the time he was 13. He was 26 when he gave his interview, saying he had seen a shift in knife crime trends and motives had become almost non-existent, with attacks being more "reckless" than targeted. Nathan, from St Anns said: "Growing up in a gang was just the norm. It's to do with the area, its area code. For instance you'd have St Anns, Radford and The Meadows. It's just because you're from different areas. Everybody was represented by a different colour. If you were from St Anns it was the Blood Gang, red, Meadows was blue because it's on the waterfront."
Nathan's interview came at a time when police revealed there had been 289 knife crimes in Nottinghamshire during the previous 12 months. Nathan was about 16 when he first decided to carry a knife. "I was thinking, other people were carrying knives," he said. "It was more a case of protecting myself against them. If someone pulls a knife on me, one of us is going to do something." He said nothing happened to him where he had to use a knife, but in a random attack a few years ago; someone ran past him and slashed him across the face while he was shopping in the city centre. "To

this day I still don't know who it was. You have your suspicions, but I would be just as bad as him if I was to go and retaliate." He said it wasn't worth reporting it to the police, asking: "What are they going to do? Lock them up? Some people like going to jail. I've got a friend, he loves it in jail. People have a structure and a routine in there. I'm not saying it's good at all, but some people see jail as an opportunity to eat, sleep and have banter."

Nottingham is no better and no worse than many cities of a similar size. Street gangs following the American model exist in many of our cities. Perhaps Nottingham was more vulnerable because of the large Jamaican community which was used as a hiding place by on the run Yardies.

What began as a purely black skinned problem, following the lead of New York's Gangstas, has become in Britain, a multi ethnic problem. Youths of all races are now drawn to Britain's street gangs, attracted by easy money and a perceived glamorous lifestyle.

Part 9 - The Twenty First Century

Chapter 9.1
Emo, "the suicide cult"

Emo is another genre of Rock music, this time characterised by its emphasis on emotional expression. It emerged out of the mid 1980s Hardcore Punk movement in Washington, where it was known as Emotional Hardcore or Emocore. Emo entered mainstream culture during the early 2000s with the success of Jimmy Eat World and Dashboard Confessional, when many Emo bands were signed by major record labels. During the mid to late 2000s, Emo bands like My Chemical Romance, Fall Out Boy and the Red Jumpsuit Apparatus became popular.

As well as being a music genre, Emo also describes elements of the fans' fashion, culture and behaviour. The Emo subculture is usually associated with fans wearing skinny jeans; tight, short sleeved t-shirts (often with the names of Emo bands), studded belts and flat, straight, jet-black hair. Emo has also been associated with the stereotypes of emotion, sensitivity, shyness, introversion and angst. It has also been connected with depression, self harm and suicide. Lyrics are typically emotional and personal, dealing with topics such as failed romance. *AllMusic* described Emo lyrics as "usually either free-associative poetry or intimate confessionals." According to *AllMusic*, early Emo bands were Hardcore Punk bands who "favoured expressive vocals over the typical barking rants" of regular Hardcore Punk.

The *New York Times* described Emo as "Emotional Punk. That is, Punk that wears its heart on its sleeve and tries a little tenderness to ease its sonic attack. If it helps, imagine Ricky Nelson singing in the Sex Pistols."

The *Los Angeles Times* said "Emo songs are mostly about pain. They are like middle-of-the-night journal entries exposing insecurity and suicidal thoughts. Or wanting the girl and even getting the girl, then going down under a swarm of conflicts and self-inflicted wounds and losing the girl to mopey confusion."

Accounts of the origins of the word Emo vary, dependent on which side of the Atlantic you live. It dates back to at least 1985. Possibly to a 1985 article in *Thrasher* magazine referring to Embrace and a few other Washington bands as; Emo-Core, which the author called "the stupidest fucking thing I've ever heard in my entire life." Over here, the *Oxford English Dictionary* dates the earliest usage of Emo-Core to 1992, with Emo first appearing in print in *New Musical Express* in 1995.

As the Emo movement spread across America, local bands began to emulate its sound to merge Hardcore Punk with the emotions of growing older. Emo combined the fatalism of The Smiths' music with Hardcore Punk. Emocore in the late 1980s remained more-or-less the same: with over-the-top lyrics about feelings sung to dramatic but decidedly Punk music.

Other Emo leaning Punk bands soon followed suit and the word Emo began to lose its vagueness and refer to romantic, emotionally overbearing music, quite distant from the political nature of Punk Rock.

The most influential Emo album of the 1990s actually came to be hated by its creator. Weezer's debut album went multi-platinum. But their 1996 follow up album, *Pinkerton*, had a darker, more abrasive sound. Frontman Rivers Cuomo's songs focused on messy, manipulative sex and his insecurity about dealing with his own celebrity. The album was a critical and commercial failure, which Rolling Stone called, "the second-worst album of the year." Cuomo retreated from the public eye, later referring to the album as "hideous" and "a hugely painful mistake." However, *Pinkerton* appealed to young people who identified with its confessional lyrics and theme of rejection. Sales grew steadily through word of mouth and online message boards. Perhaps because no one was paying attention, *Pinkerton* became the most important Emo album of the decade. Weezer returned in 2000 with a more Pop-oriented sound. Cuomo refused to play songs from Pinkerton, calling it "ugly" and "embarrassing." However, the album maintained its appeal and achieved good sales and critical praise for introducing Emo to a mainstream audience.

Emo broke into the mainstream media during the summer of 2002, when Jimmy Eat World's *Bleed American* album went platinum. Then, Dashboard Confessional reached number 22 in America with

Screaming Infidelities making them the first non-platinum-selling artists to appear on MTV Unplugged.

In the wake of this success, many Emo bands were signed by major record labels and the genre became marketable. According to Dreamworks Records senior A&R representative Luke Wood, "The industry looked at Emo as the new Rap Rock, or the new Grunge. I don't think that anyone is listening to the music, they're thinking of how they're going to take advantage of the sound's popularity at retail."

Other Emo bands which achieved mainstream success during the 2000s included My Chemical Romance, Fall Out Boy, AFI, The Red Jumpsuit Apparatus, Boys Like Girls, Panic! at the Disco and Paramore. My Chemical Romance's second album, *Three Cheers for Sweet Revenge*, went platinum in 2005.

During the 2000s, Emo fashion changed from being clean cut to more Punk. Emo fashion originally tended towards geek chic, with V-neck jumpers, white dress shirts and tight, cuffed jeans. *The Advertiser* described Emo fashion as sweaters, tight shirts, horn-rimmed glasses (like those worn by Buddy Holly), dyed black hair and fitted flat-front jeans. As Emo entered the mainstream and became a subculture, Emo fashion moved to skinny jeans, tight T-shirts (often with the names of Emo bands), studded belts, Converse sneakers, Vans and black wristbands. Thick, horn-rimmed glasses remained in style, along with eyeliner and black fingernails appearing during the mid 2000s. The best-known element of Emo fashion is its hairstyle: flat, straight, usually jet-black hair with long bangs covering much of the face.

The Emo culture has been associated with strong emotions, including: sensitivity, shyness, introversion or angst. Other stereotypes include depression, self-harm and suicide. In fact, at her inquest, the Coroner blamed Emo music for the suicide by hanging of 13 year old Hannah Bond. Emo music reportedly glamorised suicide; Hannah's obsession with My Chemical Romance was said to be linked to her death. It was said at the inquest that she was part of an Internet Emo Cult and showed an image of an Emo girl with slashed wrists on her Bebo page.

Two weeks before her death, Hannah started following American band My Chemical Romance. One of their songs contains the lyrics: "Although you're dead and gone, believe me your memory will go on."

Coroner Roger Sykes said that Hannah's death was "not glamorous, just simply a tragic loss of a young life".

Hannah's mother Heather told the inquest she had researched the trend since her daughter's death. "There are websites that show pink teddies hanging themselves," she said. "Hannah called Emo a fashion and I thought it was normal." She added: "Hannah was a normal girl. She had lots of friends. She could be a bit moody but I thought it was just because she was a teenager."

Hannah's father Ray, a karate teacher, said: "Two weeks before, I saw the cuts. I asked her about them and she said it was an Emo initiation. "She promised me she would never do it again."

Hannah used the name Living Disaster for her page on social networking website Bebo. Her page was decorated with a picture of an Emo girl with bloody wrists after slashing herself. Another picture showed a child's exercise book scrawled with the words: "Dear Diary, today I give up. . ."

The inquest in Maidstone, Kent, heard that Hannah had been with her boyfriend at a friend's house on the evening of September 22nd 2008. She had become angry when told she was not allowed to sleep over and when she got home, she went straight to her room, saying: "I want to kill myself." Her parents found that Hannah had hung herself from her bunk bed with a tie.

The inquest was told Hannah had not used drugs or alcohol before her death but Vanessa Everett, her head teacher, said self-harm had become commonplace among other Emo fans. Recording a verdict of suicide, Mr Sykes said: "The Emo overtones concerning death and associating it with glamour I find very disturbing."

Another 13 year old, Sam Leeson, committed suicide in 2008. His death was also blamed on the Emo culture. Sam's death differed from that of Hannah Bond, as Sam's death appeared to have been triggered by bullying.

Sam Leeson, who also wore the black clothes of the darkly emotional Rock genre, was also found hanging in his bedroom. Classmates and relatives said he was targeted online via his Bebo webpage because of his "alternative dress" and involvement with the Emo scene. Sam's mother, Sally Cope, said her son was a "huge" music fan with a taste for Emo-style bands, but that he also liked The Foo Fighters. She said: "He was into his appearance and often wore his black skinny jeans. He was an alternative dresser and I think other teenagers did make comments about that."

His oldest sister, Emma, aged 22, said: "We now think there has been some name-calling about the Emo thing. We know some bullying has been going on and we are disgusted and angry about it. We do not want to attack the school as they have been very good, but we are very upset it has come to this."

Ms Cope called for social networking sites like Bebo to be more strictly vetted for malicious comments.

Sam's death came only one month after the suicide of 13 year old Hannah Bond. Although there have been reports of suicide clusters with teenagers, these two deaths were not geographically close. Hanna lived in Kent, while Sam was from Gloucester.

One of the most successful of these "suicide cult" bands is My Chemical Romance. They distanced themselves from the self harm and suicide as ideals, but their first single, *Welcome to the Black Parade*, released in 2006, refers to the nickname for the place where Emo fans believe they will go when they die.

The genre experienced a backlash in response to its rapid growth. Some bands, such as Panic! at the Disco and My Chemical Romance, rejected the Emo label because of its social stigma and controversy. The backlash intensified, with *Time* magazine reporting in 2008 that anti Emo groups attacked teenagers in Mexico. Legislation was proposed in Russia's Duma (parliament) regulating Emo websites. There was also widespread banning of Emo clothing in Russian schools and government buildings. The Russians viewed the subculture as a "dangerous teen trend, promoting anti-social behaviour, depression, social withdrawal and suicide." The BBC reported that in 2012, Shia militias in Iraq shot or beat to death as many as 58 young Iraqi Emos.

Chapter 9.2
Chavs

I have included a chapter on the Chavs, because it has become
such a well used term in 21st century England. But it is quite
different to the other youth cultures covered in this book. For a start,
it is not directly connected to any musical trend, although those
fitting the visual stereotype often favour Gangsta Rap. The image
also crosses several of the earlier youth cultures, with some fitting
into the football hooligan culture and others tending more towards
the Hip Hop image. Many commentators have argued that the term
has more to do with class than culture.

A BBC TV documentary suggested that Chav culture was an
evolution of previous working class youth subcultures associated
with particular commercial clothing styles, such as Mods,
Skinheads, and Casuals.

The description Chav is used in Britain to describe a stereotype of
anti-social youth dressed in sportswear. Opinion is divided about the
origin of the term. Some suggest that Chav may have its origins in
the Romani word chavi, meaning child. The word chavvy has
existed since at least the 19th century; lexicographer Eric Partridge
mentions it in his 1950 dictionary of slang and unconventional
English, giving its date of origin as 1860.

The word in its current use is recorded by the Oxford English
Dictionary as being first used in a Usenet forum in 1998 and first
printed in a newspaper during 2002. By 2005 the term had become

widely used for a type of anti-social, uncultured youth, who wears a lot of flashy jewellery, white trainers, baseball caps, and fake designer clothes. The stereotype Chav girls tend to expose a lot of midriff, usually complemented by tattoos and piercings.

In his 2010 book *Stab Proof Scarecrows*, Lance Manley suggested that Chav was an abbreviation for Council Housed And Violent. But this is widely regarded as a backronym, or constructed acronym created to fit an existing word.

As far back as the 90s, when I joined the police, we had a name for this same group stereotype. It was based on the US military term; SNAFU, short for Situation Normal, All Fouled (or F##ked) Up. Long before I joined, the local Bobbies had amended it to describe the criminals they dealt with every day. They called them Snafs, short for; Sub Normal and F##king Useless.

Driven by websites like Chavscum and Chavtowns, the word Chav was soon adopted by the mainstream media. The base word has also mutated into "chavtastic", "chavsters", "chavette", "chavdom". Besides referring to their loutish behaviour, violence, and common speech patterns, the Chav stereotype includes wearing (often fake) branded designer sportswear, which may be accompanied by flashy gold jewellery otherwise known as Bling. They often adopt "black culture", and use some Jamaican patois in their slang.

The media picked up on the Chavs, in much the same way as they picked up on other youth trends. But TV comedians also chose to lampoon the Chavs in a way they had rarely done before. Probably the most famous of their comedy creations was the character created by Matt Lucas for the BBC show *Little Britain*. His character Vicky Pollard is a teenage girl intended to parody a Chav. He must have got something right, as a 2006 survey by YouGov suggested 70% of TV industry professionals believed that Vicky Pollard was an accurate reflection of white working class youth.

The mainstream news media combined the Chav stereotype with Matt Lucas' character when covering a 2005 anti social behaviour story. In a case where a teenage woman was barred from her own home under an anti-social behaviour order, some national newspapers branded her "the real life Vicky Pollard" with the *Daily Star* running headlines reading, "Good riddance to Chav scum: real life Vicky Pollard evicted."

In 2006, Prince William and his younger brother Prince Harry dressed up as Chavs, resulting in headlines in *The Sun* naming him "Future Bling of England". The article stated, "William has a great sense of humour and went to a lot of trouble thinking up what to wear."

In deciding what to wear for their fancy dress, the Prince's would have very quickly hit on Burberry Check. This distinctive brown check pattern has become the trademark of the Chavs and the Burberry Company's most widely copied trademark. Established in 1856 by Thomas Burberry, the company originally focused on manufacturing outdoor attire, where it had some very esteemed clients, before moving into the high fashion market. In 1911 the company became the official outfitters for Roald Amundsen, the first man to reach the South Pole, and Ernest Shackleton, who led a

1914 expedition to cross Antarctica. A Burberry Gabardine jacket was also worn by George Mallory on his attempt to climb Mount Everest in 1924. Adapted to meet the needs of soldiers, the Trench Coat was developed by Burberry during WWI. The name Trench Coat coming from its use by British officers in the trenches. After the war, it also became popular with civilians. The iconic brown Burberry check has been in use since at least the 1920s, primarily as a lining in its trench coats.

Burberry was an independent family company until 1955, when Great Universal Stores assumed ownership.

Between 2001 and 2005, Burberry became linked to Chav and Football Hooligan culture. This change in the brand reputation was attributed to the proliferation of counterfeit goods adopting Burberry's trademark check pattern and its adoption by celebrities prominently identified with Chav culture. The association with Football Hooliganism led to some venues banning the wearing of Burberry check garments.

Great Universal Stores sold its remaining interest in Burberry in December 2005. The new Directors successfully turned around the brand's Chav like reputation by removing the check pattern from all but 10% of the company's products.

Response to the stereotype has ranged from amusement to criticism, with some saying that it is a new manifestation of classism. *The Guardian* in 2011 commented on issues stemming from the use of the terms "Hoodies" and "Chav" within the mass media. They claimed this had led to age discrimination as a result of mass media-created stereotypes.

In his 2011 book, *Chavs: The Demonisation of the Working Class*, Owen Jones argued that the word is an "attack on the poor."

In a 2005 article in *The Times*, Julie Burchill called the use of the word; a form of "social racism" and that such "sneering" reveals more about the shortcomings of the "Chav-haters" than those of their victims. The writer John Harris argued along similar lines in a 2007 article in *The Guardian*.

The more left-leaning commentators describe it as a way of bashing the poor. In 2008 the Fabian Society urged the BBC to add it to their list of offensive terms. "This is middle class hatred of the white working class, pure and simple," wrote Tom Hampsen, the Society's Editorial Director. He also called on the Commission for Equality and Human Rights to take this kind of class discrimination seriously. But, there are plenty of people for whom the word is harmless. *Daily Telegraph* blogger James Delingpole, for example, argued it was merely an updating of "oik".

In 2008, there was a bizarre and rare turnaround in cross culture violence. Where Goths have usually been a culture of victims, Terry Sewell kicked another teenager to death in a drunken attack and then told friends: "Don't worry, it's just a Chav."

Violent Goth, Terry Sewell and his friend Darren Abrams, both aged 20, attacked 19 year old Jed Sheridan after a night out drinking. Abrams smashed a bottle over Sheridan's head and Sewell repeatedly kicked him in the head as he lay on the ground. The second kick flipped Sheridan over on to his back, banging his head on the Tarmac.

Paramedics spotted the small cut on his head but Sheridan refused to go to hospital, insisting he just wanted to go to sleep. The ambulance took him to his home in nearby Portsmouth, where he died in his sleep. He had a fractured skull, a haemorrhage which put pressure on his brain and extensive bruising and swelling of the brain.

Prosecutor Timothy Mousley QC said that the next day Sewell, who called himself a Goth, bragged to friends that he had stamped on a man's head. Mr Mousley said: "Sewell was not upset for Jed Sheridan because he had a strong disliking for Chavs." Sewell had told police he was in a gang, the TSE Crew, which went around beating up Chavs.

Jailing Sewell for life Mr Justice Roderick Evans said: "This was mindless, drunken violence. You and Darren Abrams had an unhealthy interest in fighting. It is the kind of stupid violence decent people see as a blight on towns and cities."

Chapter 9.3
Hipsters

The most current of youth trends appears just as ridiculous to this 50 year old author as the Punks and New Romantics seemed in my younger days. The Hipsters are the ones people are making fun of with their checked shirts, fixed gear bicycles, avocado on toast and full beards.

Like many youth cultures, it all started in America, or more precisely in Brooklyn. Throughout most of the 20th century, Brooklyn was working class, but in the 1990s, better off people arrived fleeing the high rents of Manhattan. After that the borough became a destination of choice for young non-conformists and artists.

The stereotypical Hipster subculture is composed of young whites who live mainly in gentrifying urban neighbourhoods. It is usually associated with indie and alternative music. Hipsters also favour non-mainstream fashion, wearing vintage and charity shop-bought clothing; generally they favour green political views, veganism, organic and artisanal foods, alternative lifestyles and snobbery.

A slightly tongue in cheek internet guide to being a Hipster explained how to look the part. "Dress in Vintage; If there are any brand-name items of clothing in your closet, get rid of them. A true Hipster strays from all that is "mainstream." So, take the road less travelled and hit your local thrift shops. Wear Wayfarer Glasses; Whether you need glasses or not, your Hipster look is not complete without a pair of groovy wayfarer glasses. The thicker the frames, the better. When it comes to dressing like a Hipster, shoes are just as important as your overall ensemble. To play it safe (and retro) invest in a used pair of Converse, that are at least 15 years old. The key is that your shoes must look worn out. Remember that you are trying to be unique not Emo, so have several pairs of shoes to style your look. Accessorise; add a chunky, knitted scarf or a colourful beanie. Bags are big, with a cross strap like a messenger bag."

The term Hipster in its current use first appeared in the 1990s. But its origins come from the term used to describe the earlier movements of the 1940s Jazz Age, when "hip" was as an adjective to describe aficionados of the growing scene, who were "hip" or "in the know".

Members of the subculture today do not self-identify as Hipsters, and the word Hipster is often used as mockery to describe someone who is pretentious or overly trendy. In 2012, Berlin began holding the Hipster Olympics, an event that pokes fun at Hipster fashion with competitions such as the Cloth Bag Sack Race and the Horn-Rimmed Glasses Throw.

Ridiculing young poseurs is not an especially new thing to do. The Guardian's Charlie Brooker created the character of Nathan Barley, a media playboy, back in 1999. Around the same time east London fanzine; The Shoreditch Twat published its first edition. Many of the jokes in 80s sitcom The Young Ones were at the expense of such youthful pretentions.

The Hipster Handbook described Brooklyn Hipsters as young

people with "mop-top haircuts, swinging retro pocketbooks, talking on cell phones, smoking European cigarettes, strutting in platform shoes with a biography of Che Guevara sticking out of their bags". But a similar phenomenon was happening in Britain, with young workers in the media and digital industries moving into historically working class areas of London such as Spitalfields and Shoreditch. Long forgotten styles of clothing, beer, cigarettes and music were becoming popular again. Retro was cool and old was the new 'new'. Kids began to wear cardigans and Buddy Holly glasses; they enjoyed the irony of making something so nerdy become cool. They wanted to live sustainably and eat organic gluten-free grains. Above all, they wanted to be different from the mainstream and carve a cultural niche for themselves. For this new generation, style wasn't something you could buy in a department store, it was something you found in a thrift shop, or, even better, made yourself. The way to be cool wasn't to look like a television star: it was to look like as though you'd never seen television."

The Hipsters' love of retro spilled over into cycling. Their preferred mount was the fixie, or fixed wheel bicycle, with no free wheel hub. They could be seen on these primitive, impractical devices, wobbling around at most red traffic lights in London, momentarily unbalanced by their retro satchels. The irony of it all was, that in their quest to stand out they all ended up looking the same. Some of their supposedly individual fashions became mainstream: now, even police officers can wear a beard and have tattoos.

In 2014, the *Guardian* interviewed Josh, a 30 year old artist and chef who lived in a converted warehouse in Hackney. Josh has a beard, glasses and cares about the provenance of his coffee. He pays his tax, but doesn't have a 9 to 5 job and he shuns public transport, preferring to ride a bicycle. On paper, Josh is the archetypal Hipster, just don't call him one: "I don't hate the word Hipster, but being a hipster doesn't mean anything any more. So God forbid anyone calls me one."

At some point in the last few years, the Hipster changed. Or at least its definition did. What began as an umbrella term for a counter culture tribe of young creative types in New York and Hackney morphed into a term for people, who looked, lived and acted a certain way.

Alex Miller, UK Editor of *Vice*, explains: "We've never written about Hipsters as a subculture at *Vice* because I don't think Hipsters are a subculture. However, I do appreciate that people like the idea of belonging to something, so I suppose on that level the idea exists."

British economist and former British government adviser Douglas McWilliams said, "Hipsters have inherited the golden boy ethos of the 1990s and updated it with more populist values; ostentation is now being seen as in supremely bad taste. The Ferraris and champagne of yesteryear have been replaced with Tube tickets, bicycles and cappuccinos to go." In his book, *The Flat White Economy*, McWilliams sees the phenomenon of the hip young entrepreneur as a central element in the new world economy. The success of Hipster style comes from the fact that "it isn't associated with a logo, so it can be reproduced at all levels of fashion," McWilliams said, using the example of skinny jeans and lumberjack shirts, which are as easy to find at upscale designer shops as they are at a Discount outlet. "You show that you're 'in', not by buying something with a logo on it but by your ability to follow the rush for the latest eccentricity."

In 2017 *The New York Times* reported on two men who fulfilled the Hipster desire for unorthodox boutique businesses. Paddy Screech, aged 51, is an Oxford educated Cornishman with a close trimmed beard. His friend Jonathan Privett, aged 52, is a gap toothed Yorkshireman. Neither of them wears the stereotype lumberjack shirts or full Hipster beards, but they do run London's only floating bookstore. Their business, Word on the Water, is proof that there really is something you can do with an English literature degree, other than teach English literature. The store, based in a 50 foot long canal boat, is stuffed to its bulkheads with books. It now has a permanent berth on the Regent's Canal, just around the corner from the British Library. This comes after years of its owners staying one step ahead of eviction from the canals, by relocating every fortnight. When they met, Jonathan Privett was living on a canal boat, as part of a subculture of boat dwellers who berthed on London's canals for free, as long as they kept moving periodically. Paddy Screech had been working with homeless people and drug addicts. He went for a walk, stumbled on a canal and met Jonathan. The two then cooked up the idea of the store. A French friend, Stephane Chaudat, provided a boat big enough to become the shop, a 1920s Dutch barge. Jonathan had a stock of used books. Paddy borrowed £2,000 from his mum as capital and their business was born in 2010.

Forced by the berthing laws to move every fortnight, they often found themselves on parts of the nine mile long Regent's Canal which had industrial buildings and no customers. To their surprise, they discovered they had what Paddy called "an invisible community of people silently watching us," patrons who had discovered them over the years, including some prominent authors and others who had big social media presences. As the canal trust peppered them with legal notices, fines and threats to have the boat barge lifted out of the water and broken up, their supporters went into action. Eventually the authorities gave in and agreed to give them a permanent berth just at the time the area, known as Granary Square, was being redeveloped with trendy shops and restaurants and plenty of foot traffic. A crowd funding campaign raised enough money to fund the move.

Now they run a relaxed operation, often not even monitoring customers who climb aboard the barge, but remaining in their folding lawn chairs out on the towpath. "You can't buy heroin with books," Paddy said.

Their roof has an open mic for any musician, busker or poetry reader, which can attract hundreds of willing performers.

Many people have suggested that the men sell trinkets, coffee and drinks, but they have resisted such commercialisation. "I didn't study English literature for three years to serve coffee," said Jonathan.

Where violence is found in the Hipster subculture, it is usually directed against them. In 2015 a mob of 200 anti-capitalists attacked Cereal Killer Cafe, a Hipster cafe in London which serves only cereal. The 'F*** Parade' organisers claimed the demonstration was intended to protest against unaffordable housing in East London. According to the Metropolitan Police "an element within a group of several hundred people started throwing missiles and caused criminal damage to several shops. One officer was injured when he was struck on the head by a bottle."

Gary Keery of the Cereal Killer Cafe said: ' It was intense. It wasn't expected. I couldn't believe it was happening. They had pigs heads and torches. They wrote the word 'scum'. Luckily it's all external damage. They threw paint bombs at the windows and tried to let off a smoke bomb in the shop. Inside the cafe customers and staff were forced to shelter as the mob, many of whom were masked, shouted outside."

His brother Alan said a smoke bomb and furniture were thrown inside while staff barricaded the cafe door. "It was like a witch hunt. There were people with pitchforks, pig heads and burning torches. It was like something from the Middle Ages," he said. "It was a bunch of anarchists who claimed to represent the poor people of East London and it's ridiculous. They were all boozing in the streets; there was a lot of obscenity."

The protesters also broke the window of a nearby estate agent. According to Mr Keery there was no advanced warning of the attack. He said: "They claimed to be protesting about gentrification, but they attacked a small business owned by two working class lads from Belfast."

The anarchists warned that "Hipsters beware" as they advertised their so-called F*** Parade. A statement on their website claimed: "We don't want luxury flats that no one can afford, we want genuinely affordable housing. We don't want Pop-up gin bars or brioche buns; we want community. Soon this city will be an unrecognisable, bland, yuppie-infested wasteland with no room for normal people like us."

Their website also said that "The past F*** Parades have been fun and furious with music, pyrotechnics and cheeky banner drops. They brought together hundreds of revellers, Ravers and wrong-un's and were reported widely in the media."

Conclusions

I have thoroughly enjoyed doing the research for this, my first non fiction offering. I hope you enjoy reading it just as much. I can not pretend this book has been a serious academic research project, as I have selected stories I found interesting, rather than for their academic value. But through the depth of my reading, I have formed some opinions on the things I have read.

It seems inevitable that sections of our youth will set themselves apart as separate cultures. Popular opinion puts the advent of a Rock & Roll as the beginning of the teenager and the first youth culture. This is only partially true, as my book gives examples from the 19th century as well as the 1920s and 40s, long before Bill Haley arrived in Britain.

There were many factors that made the 1950s different to the decades which went before. The working week was becoming shorter, giving the working class young more free time. Credit was only just becoming available to the young, enabling them to buy motorcycles, scooters and fancy clothes. A more prevalent media also played a big part in spreading word of the youth cultures in the 50s and 60s, with cinema and newspapers more widely available.

When I say youth culture was inevitable, I refer to humanity at its most basic. As a species we like to think of ourselves as very sophisticated, evolutionary advanced from every other animal around us. But, while our ability to communicate does give us a very large advantage, in evolutionary terms we are still pack animals. As with any pack, there is a very delicate hierarchy, with everyone either accepting their place, or vying to improve their position. Whatever the case, we all have an evolutionary need to be accepted at some level.

In the teenager, you can add to this basic of human nature; out of control hormones and the angst of growing up. There can be little wonder that our youngsters form themselves into packs of their own.

Another factor which appears to have had a big impact on our youth cultures is the cult of celebrity. This is something which has increased as technology improved the proliferation of both the music and the opinions of popular artists.

As with any generalisation, there are exceptions, such as Sting, who was a school teacher, before finding fame as front man of The Police. But in general, Pop singers are not known for their great intellect, yet big sections of our society hang on their every word and opinion.

For example, before researching this book, I did not know that at the beginning of the Skinhead subculture, there were both black and white youngsters attaching themselves to the culture. In the melting pot of inner city London, white youths took a liking to the music and culture of the new West Indian immigrants. Then, the newly successful black artists decided to add politics to their music, singing about Black Nationalism and Rastafarianism. It did not take long for the working class white to separate themselves from this trend and before long, the National Front were making overtures to the Skinheads.

The news media, which as a Member of the Chartered Institute of Journalists, I include myself, have a lot to answer for. Virtually every subculture I have studied had been played up, or misrepresented in some form or other.

The fights between Mods and Rockers had quite minor beginnings, before sensational stories appeared on the front pages of national newspapers. These stories drew yet more youngsters to our seaside towns, seeking their own piece of the action.

I only found two widely reported examples of the Emo subculture being directly linked to suicide and one of them was the result of bullying. Yet the news reports of the time categorically blamed their culture for the deaths. One of the reports even called My Chemical Romance, "a suicide cult band." I almost deleted the reference from that chapter of my book, but decided to leave it in, to make this point.

The media has also given oxygen to the Gangsta Rappers, in glorifying their homage to guns, violence and drug dealing. Then when tragedy struck and young Danielle Beccan was shot as a result of her gang associations, the media completely failed in issuing any warning to other youngsters. If the community of St Annes had shunned the Gangstas, rather than admiring them, many youngsters might still be alive.

If I can suggest one thing that everyone could do to focus our youngsters pack instincts in a positive direction, it is to give a little of their time. The TV swallows increasing amounts of our time, while the youngsters either play on computers, or entertain themselves. It is much more productive to find a few common interests with your kids, while they are young enough to accept them.

Many of us feel good about ourselves by texting to give money to any of the high profile TV campaigns. Why not volunteer a little of your time instead? There are many Scout, Guide, Cadet, or sports groups which desperately need adult help. If activity is not your thing, there are also arts groups to get involved with. Part of Danielle Beccan's legacy is to fund a music and dance club in St Anns.

When Prince Harry and his then fiancée Meghan Markle visited the Nottingham Academy soon after their engagement in 2017, it was good to see both black and white kids involved in the school's Hip Hop club. I just hope the focus is on its early use in New York, as none violent competition between the gangs.

If you enjoyed reading Rocking the Streets, please read my next non-fiction offering

Mofos: a history of British Biker Culture

Stone, Paper, Bomb

A Nev Stone & The Watchers MC Adventure

Nev Stone's second adventure takes him and the Watchers to the Americas, where a fanatical sect plans to detonate an improvised nuclear device in the United States, blaming Islamic terrorists.

The action moves between England, Portugal, Cuba and New Orleans as the bikers track the players and the nuclear components. Time is against them as they race to prevent a bigger catastrophe than 9/11.

Breath Becomes Stone

A Nev Stone & The Watchers MC Adventure

Nev Stone & the Watchers third adventure takes them to New Zealand.

Disgraced ex cop, Nev Stone now works with the Watchers MC and their global security business. Contracting for MI6, they are sent undercover to New Zealand, where smuggling of rare animals has caught the attention of Britain's Royal Family. The action moves through Hong Kong, China and New Zealand, as the Watchers fight environmental disaster.

Loxley: A dish served cold

A modern day Robin Hood tale.

Major Robin Loxley returns from the Middle East to attend his father's funeral and take on his duties as Duke of Loxley. Estranged from the old Duke for many years, this is Robin's first return to Sherwood since the death of his mother.

Robin learns that the old duke has mortgaged Loxley Hall to fund a lifestyle of drink, drugs, gambling and women. With the death of the Duke, the holder of his debt calls in the mortgage. This pits Robin and his Special Forces team against Nottingham's shadowy drug lord known as the Tax Collector. Vowing never to use guns on the streets of their city, Robin's Outlaws use historic weapons to tear down the Tax Collector's empire.

The Tricycle Spy

(Coming Soon)

A biographical novel, based on my father's lifetime fight against communism.

Gordon Hallam first worked with Special Branch as a young soldier in the Malayan Emergency. On leaving the Army, Gordon joined the police, serving in Traffic and CID, before again working with Special Branch in England.

A crippling stroke ended Gordon's police career, but it did not end his involvement with Special Branch. Now disabled and riding a tricycle, Gordon's former collegues put him back to work as an undercover agent. This time Gordon was spying on left wing subversives, trying to make a toe hold for communism in Britain.

A non-fiction title

Mofos:

A history of British Biker Culture

This project started several years ago. There are lots of books on American Motorcycle Cubs, usually sensationalised with the label biker gangs. But the biker subculture in England had very different origins, as the Teddy Boys evolved into Rockers, before eventually adopting the three part patch used by the American clubs.

I missed the early days of the 1950s and early 60s, but I have lived though most of the developments in the English biker scene.

With a mix of first hand accounts and academic research, this book will be my take on a subculture in which I have spent many happy years.

Printed in Great Britain
by Amazon

36321175R00148